Cover Photograph: U.S. Fish and Wildlife Service

The mission of the U.S. Fish & Wildlife Service is working with others to conserve, protect, and enhance fish and wildlife and their habitats for the continuing benefit of the American people.

The mission of the National Wildlife Refuge System is to administer a national network of lands and waters for the conservation, management and, where appropriate, restoration of the fish, wildlife and plant resources and their habitats within the United States for the benefit of present and future generations of Americans.

Comprehensive Conservation Plans provide long-term guidance for management decisions; set forth goals, objectives and strategies needed to accomplish refuge purposes; and, identify the Fish and Wildlife Service's best estimate of future needs. These plans detail program planning levels that are sometimes substantially above current budget allocations and, as such, are primarily for Service strategic planning and program prioritization purposes. The plans do not constitute a commitment for staffing increases, operational and maintenance increases, or funding for future land acquisition.

Rice Lake and Mille Lacs

National Wildlife Refuges

Comprehensive Conservation Plan Approval

Submitted by:

Walt Ford   9/19/2007

Walt Ford   Date
Refuge Manager

Concur:

James T. Leach   11-29-07

James T. Leach   Date
Refuge Supervisor, Area 3

Nita M. Fuller   11·30·2007

Nita M. Fuller   Date
Regional Chief, National Wildlife Refuge System

Approve:

           Charles M. Wooley
           Acting Regional Director

Charlie Wooley   12/4/07

Robyn Thorson   Date
Regional Director

for

Rice Lake and Mille Lacs

National Wildlife Refuges

Comprehensive Conservation Plan

List of Figures

List of Tables

Chapter 1: Introduction and Background

Introduction

This document is a comprehensive conservation plan (CCP) for Rice Lake National Wildlife Refuge (NWR) and Mille Lacs NWR in east-central Minnesota. Both refuges are administered by the staff at Rice Lake NWR. Because the administration of the refuges draws from the same resources, it makes sense to consider their management together.

Mille Lacs NWR is the smallest refuge in the National Wildlife Refuge System, which includes more than 545 refuges. The 0.57-acre Refuge consists of two islands, Hennepin and Spirit, in Mille Lacs Lake, and is about 30 air miles southwest of the Rice Lake NWR office (Figure 1). The islands are covered with jumbled rock, boulders, and gravel. Hennepin Island is managed as a nesting colony for the State-listed threatened Common Tern. Spirit Island is used by other colonial nesting species including Ring-billed Gulls, Herring Gulls, and Double-crested Cormorants.

The 20,253-acre Rice Lake NWR is a mosaic of lakes, marshes, forests, and grasslands that provide a variety of habitats for migrant and resident wildlife. Abundant natural foods, particularly wild rice, have attracted wildlife to the area for centuries. The Refuge is especially noted for its fall concentrations of Ring-necked Ducks, which often number over 150,000 birds. Other important migrants include Mallards, Wood Ducks, Canvasback, Canada Geese, and Woodcock. White-tailed deer, black bear, river otter, beaver, Sandhill Cranes, Bald Eagles, Ruffed and Sharptail Grouse inhabit the Refuge. Songbirds, raptors, and nearly all other species associated with the bogs and forests of northern Minnesota, including gray wolves and an occasional moose, are also found on the Refuge.

Rice Lake at Rice Lake NWR. USFWS

Rice Lake NWR includes the 2,045-acre parcel known as the Sandstone Unit (Unit), located approximately 40 miles southeast of the main part of the Refuge near the town of Sandstone, Minnesota. The majority of the Unit is upland forest with smaller components of grassland, forested wetland, shallow marshes, bogs, and riverine wetlands. The State-designated Wild and Scenic Kettle River traverses the west side of the Unit, creating spectacular bluffs and rock outcroppings. The State and Aitkin County manage significant lands in the vicinity of Rice Lake NWR. Figure 2 illustrates these conservation lands that have both wildlife and recreational value.

In the following sections we present our organizational, legal, and policy background. Then, we describe the establishment of the Refuge, its history, purpose, vision, and goals. In Chapter 2 we describe the process we used in planning. Chapter 3 describes the Refuges and our current management. In Chapter 4 we describe how we intend to manage for the next 15 years. In Chapter 5 we

Figure 1: Location of Rice Lake NWR and Mille Lac NWR

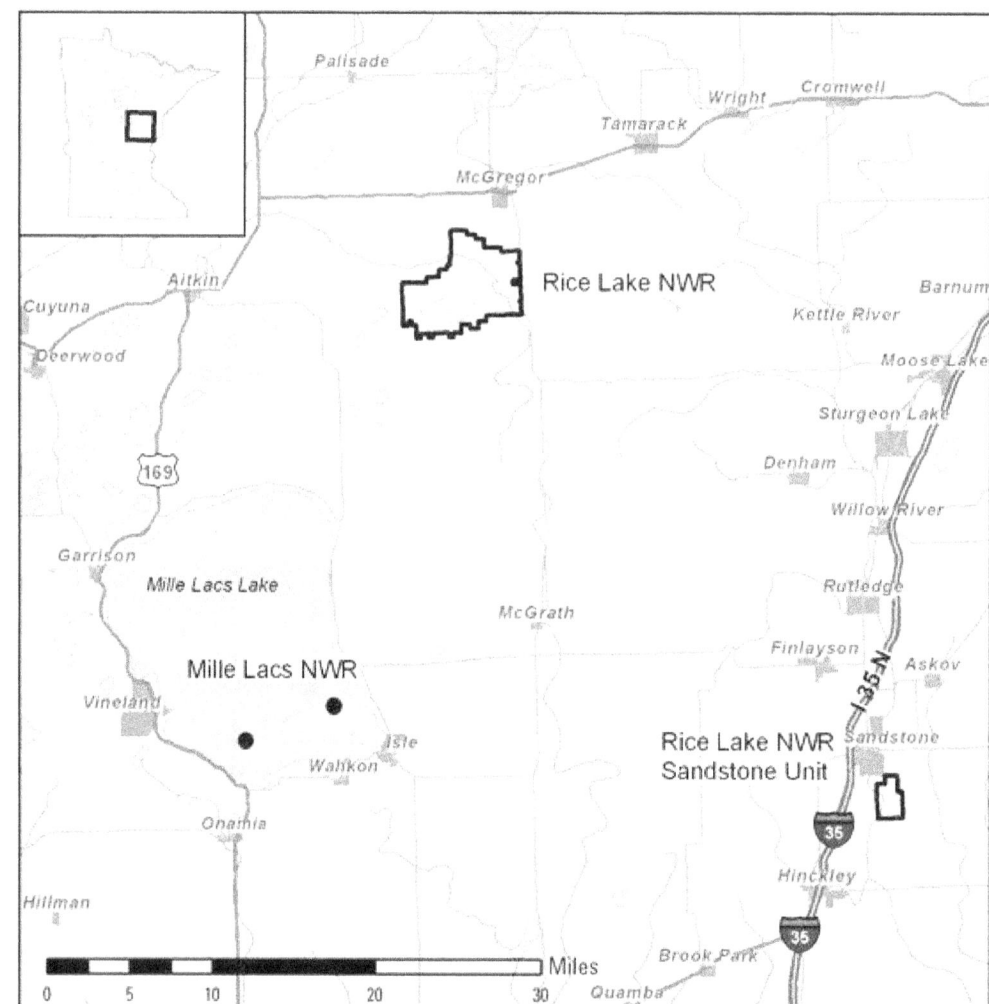

describe how we expect to accomplish our plan in terms of projects, staff, and more detailed planning. We use the appendices to present detailed information not included in our narrative.

The U.S. Fish and Wildlife Service

The Refuge is administered by the U.S. Fish and Wildlife Service (Service), the primary federal agency responsible for conserving, protecting, and enhancing the nation's fish and wildlife populations and their habitats. The Service oversees the enforcement of federal wildlife laws, management

and protection of migratory bird populations, restoration of nationally significant fisheries, administration of the Endangered Species Act, and the restoration of wildlife habitat such as wetlands. The Service also manages the National Wildlife Refuge System.

Mission of the U.S. Fish and Wildlife Service

The mission of the Service is working with others to conserve, protect and enhance fish, wildlife, and plants and their habitats for the continuing benefit of the American people.

Figure 2: Conservation Lands Near Rice Lake NWR

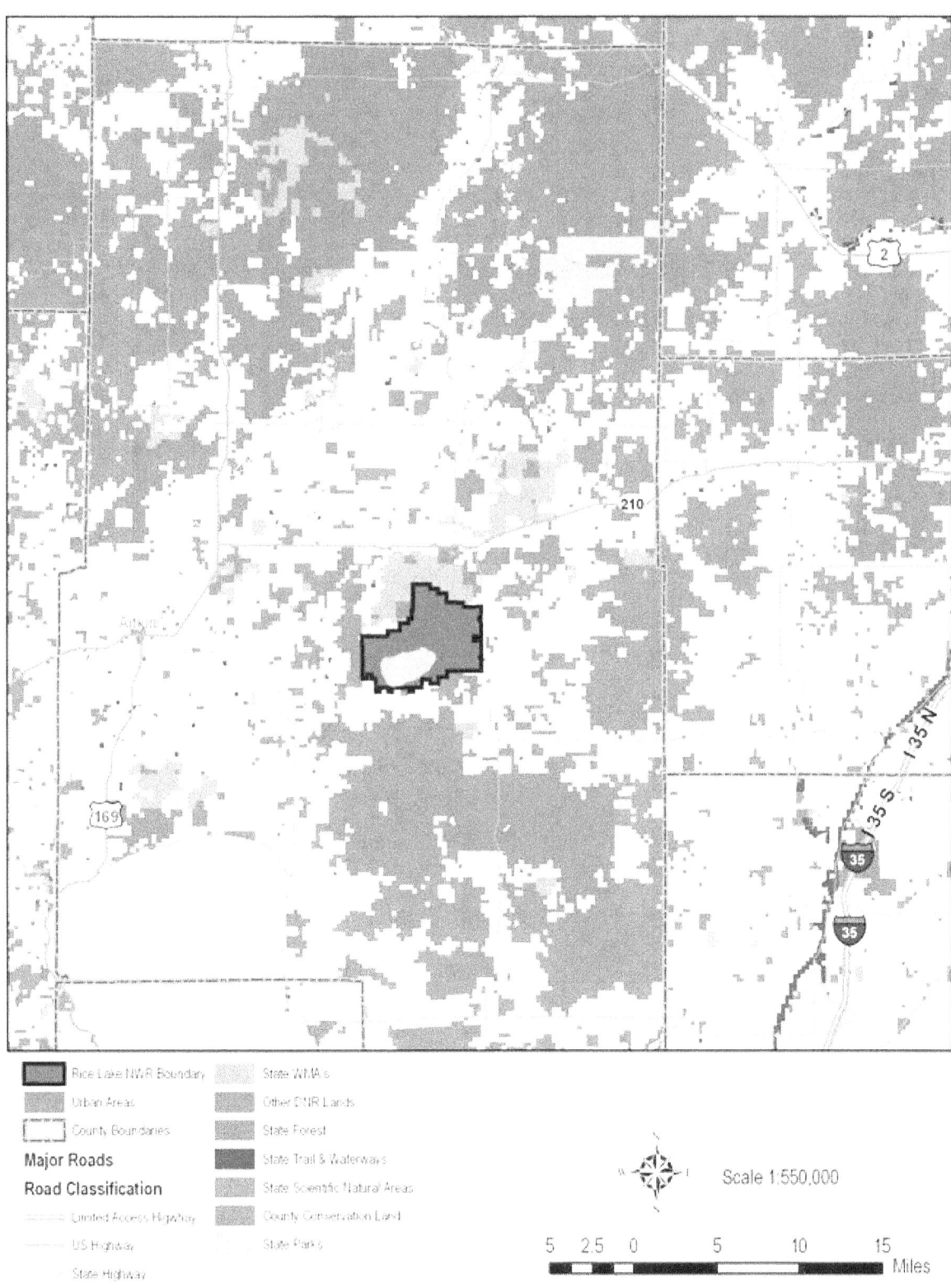

The National Wildlife Refuge System

Refuge lands are part of the National Wildlife Refuge System, which was founded in 1903 when President Theodore Roosevelt designated Pelican Island in Florida as a sanctuary for Brown Pelicans. Today, the System is a network of more than 545 refuges covering more than 95 million acres of public lands and waters. Most of these lands (82 percent) are in Alaska, with approximately 16 million acres located in the lower 48 states and several island territories. The National Wildlife Refuge System is the world's largest collection of lands specifically managed for fish and wildlife. Overall, it provides habitat for more than 5,000 species of birds, mammals, fish, and insects. As a result of international treaties for migratory bird conservation as well as other legislation, such as the Migratory Bird Conservation Act of 1929, many refuges have been established to protect migratory waterfowl and their migratory flyways, from their northern nesting grounds to their southern wintering areas. Refuges also play a vital role in preserving endangered and threatened species. Among the most notable is Aransas National Wildlife Refuge in Texas, which provides winter habitat for the Whooping Crane. Likewise, the Florida Panther Refuge protects one of the nation's most endangered predators.

Refuges also provide unique wildlife-dependent recreational opportunities for visitors. When public uses are deemed compatible with wildlife and habitat conservation, they are places where people can enjoy hunting, fishing, wildlife observation, photography, environmental education, and environmental interpretation. Many refuges have visitor centers, wildlife trails, automobile tours, and environmental education programs. Nationwide, approximately 39.5 million people visited national wildlife refuges in 2003.

Mission of the National Wildlife Refuge System

The mission of the National Wildlife Refuge System is to administer a national network of lands and waters for the conservation, management, and where appropriate, restoration of fish, wildlife, and plant resources and their habitats within the United States for the benefit of present and future generations of Americans.

Revised goals for the National Wildlife Refuge System were adopted on July 26, 2006, and incorporated into Part 601, Chapter 1, of the Fish and Wildlife Service Manual (601 FW 1). The goals are:

- Conserve a diversity of fish, wildlife, and plants and their habitats, including species that are endangered or threatened with becoming endangered.

- Develop and maintain a network of habitats for migratory birds, anadromous and interjurisdictional fish, and marine mammal populations that is strategically distributed and carefully managed to meet important life history needs of these species across their ranges.

- Conserve those ecosystems, plant communities, wetlands of national or international significance, and landscapes and seascapes that are unique, rare, declining, or underrepresented in existing protection efforts.

- Provide and enhance opportunities to participate in compatible wildlife-dependent recreation (hunting, fishing, wildlife observation and photography, and environmental education and interpretation).

- Foster understanding and instill appreciation of the diversity and interconnectedness of fish, wildlife, and plants and their habitats.

Legal and Policy Guidance

The National Wildlife Refuge System Improvement Act of 1997 established several important mandates aimed at making the management of national wildlife refuges more cohesive. The preparation of CCPs is one of those mandates. The Act directs the Secretary of the Interior to ensure that the mission of the National Wildlife Refuge System and purposes of the individual refuges are carried out. The 1997 Refuge Improvement Act requires the Secretary to maintain the biological integrity, diversity, and environmental health and to identify the archeological and cultural values of the National Wildlife Refuge System. The Act deals with compatibility of uses on refuges and directs the Secretary of Interior to issue regulations for compatibility determinations. The Act also directs that compatible wildlife-dependent uses should be facilitated. Since passage of the Act, the Service has adopted policies that implement direction of the Act.

Compatibility Policy

Service policy says that no uses for which the Service has authority to regulate may be allowed on a unit of the Refuge System unless it is determined to be compatible. A compatible use is a use that, in the sound professional judgment of the refuge manager, will not materially interfere with or detract from the fulfillment of the National Wildlife Refuge System mission or the purposes of the national wildlife refuge. Managers must complete a written compatibility determination for each use, or collection of like uses, that is signed by the manager and the Regional Chief of Refuges in the respective Service region.

Biological Integrity, Diversity, and Environmental Health Policy

The Service is directed in the Refuge Improvement Act to "ensure that the biological integrity, diversity, and environmental health of the Refuge System are maintained for the benefit of present and future generations of Americans..." The biological integrity policy helps define and clarify this directive by providing guidance on what conditions constitute biological integrity, diversity, and environmental health; guidelines for maintaining existing levels; guidelines for determining how and when it is appropriate to restore lost elements; and guidelines in dealing with external threats to biological integrity, diversity and health.

Other Guidance

In addition to the Refuges' establishing executive orders, authorizing legislation, and the National Wildlife Refuge System Improvement Act of 1997,

Coyote. USFWS

several Federal laws, executive orders, and regulations govern administration of the Refuge. Appendix C contains a partial list of the legal mandates that guided the preparation of this plan and those that pertain to Refuge management activities.

Establishment and Purposes of the Refuges

Rice Lake National Wildlife Refuge

Conservationists were concerned about low duck populations during the Dust Bowl years of the 1930s. One strategy to help the populations was to provide for and protect ducks on their southern migration. Rice Lake historically, and even during the drought years, had large populations of migrating waterfowl. Thus, the area was identified as one of the first to be purchased in an attempt to stem the decline of waterfowl populations.

Franklin D. Roosevelt established Rice Lake Migratory Waterfowl Refuge by Executive Order in 1935 "as a refuge and breeding ground for migratory birds and other wildlife." Following initial land purchases, using NIR Wildlife Refuges Funds (also known as the $6 Million Fund) and Duck Stamp Funds, early development of the Refuge was accomplished using Civilian Conservation Corps labor (Camp BS-3, Company 2705). A Presidential proclamation changed the name of the Refuge to Rice Lake National Wildlife Refuge in 1940.

The Sandstone Unit (Unit) was initially acquired by the United States in 1932 for the purpose of establishing a federal prison. The Department of Justice, Bureau of Prisons, administered the Sandstone Federal Correctional Institution (FCI) on a portion of the original 2,885-acre acquisition from 1939 to 1949 and again from 1959 until the present. In 1969, the Department of Justice declared 2,405 acres of the FCI surplus to their needs. On February 18, 1970, 2,240 acres were transferred to the Department of Interior for inclusion within the National Wildlife Refuge System. In April 1986, the Service transferred 195 acres of the Unit to the City of Sandstone as part of a three-way exchange between the City of Sandstone, the Minnesota Department of Natural Resources (DNR), and the Fish and Wildlife Service. Total area for the Unit is currently 2,045 acres.

Lands for Rice Lake NWR were acquired under the original Executive Order, The Migratory Bird Conservation Act, the Refuge Recreation Act, and An Act Authorizing the Transfer of Certain Real Property for Wildlife and Other Purposes. The authority of An Act Authorizing the Transfer of Certain Real Property for Wildlife and Other Purposes was used to transfer the Sandstone Unit from the Department of Justice to the Fish and Wildlife Service.

Service policy states that when refuge land is acquired it takes on the purpose of its acquisition authority plus the purposes outlined in the authorities used to acquire previous land for the same refuge. The Refuge's purposes thus include:

- "a refuge and breeding ground for migratory birds and other wildlife" (Executive Order 7221).

- "an inviolate sanctuary, or for any other management purpose, for migratory birds" (Migratory Bird Conservation Act).

- "(1) incidental fish and wildlife-oriented recreational development, (2) the protection of natural resources, (3) the conservation of endangered species or threatened species" (Refuge Recreation Act).

- "carrying out the national migratory bird management program" (An Act Authorizing the Transfer of Certain Real Property for Wildlife, or Other Purposes).

- "... for the development, advancement, management, conservation, and protection of fish and wildlife resources ..." 16 U.S.C. § 742f(a)(4) "... for the benefit of the United States Fish and Wildlife Service, in performing its activities and services. Such acceptance may be subject to the terms of any restrictive or affirmative covenant, or condition of servitude ..." 16 U.S.C. § 742f(b)(1) (Fish and Wildlife Act of 1956).

Mille Lacs National Wildlife Refuge

The two islands that make up Mille Lacs NWR were given national designation in separate orders. Woodrow Wilson set aside Spirit Island with Executive Order 2199 on May 14, 1915, as Mille Lacs Reservation. On October 13, 1920, Wilson enlarged the reservation by the addition of Hennepin Island under Executive Order 3340. The two islands were to constitute a "preserve and breeding ground for native birds" – its purpose. In the very same 1940

proclamation that renamed Rice Lake Migratory Waterfowl Refuge as Rice Lake NWR, Mille Lacs Reservation was changed to Mille Lacs National Wildlife Refuge, located within the boundaries of Mille Lacs Indian Reservation (Figure 3).

Refuge Vision

The vision for the Refuge provides a simple statement of the desired future condition of the Refuge. From the vision flow more specific goals that lead to even more detailed and measurable objectives. We considered the purposes of the Refuges and the mission of the System as we envisioned what Rice Lake NWR could offer future generations of wildlife and people. Our visions for the refuges are:

Rice Lake National Wildlife Refuge

Rice Lake NWR will be an area treasured by neighbors and visitors alike for its bountiful wild rice, clean water, well-managed forests, abundant wildlife and wildlife recreational opportunities. A towering canopy of red and white pine will intermingle with aspen stands, majestic old growth oak forests, and tamarack-spruce bogs. This mosaic of northern forest types will support a great diversity of neotropical migrants, mammals and unique plant species. The bogs will be free of invasive brush species and home to countless marshbirds, amphibians and species not commonly seen. Rice Lake will be the prominent natural wild rice producing lake in the state. In the fall, people will be captivated by the sight of rice heads swaying in the wind as far as the eye can see and the sounds of hundreds-of-thousands of ducks, geese and swans feasting on the bounty. American Indians will hand-harvest the rice from their canoes, passing on a tradition to the next generation. Visitors will understand the importance of the Refuge, not only for the wildlife but for its history. They will feel welcome, oriented and relish the serenity at hand.

Mille Lacs National Wildlife Refuge

Mille Lacs NWR will be a cornerstone in maintaining the Common Tern population in the Great Lakes Region. Caspian Terns, Ruddy Turnstones, Sanderlings, Dunlin, Least Sandpipers, and Semipalmated Sandpipers, will continue to use this small but important Refuge for resting and feeding during their lengthy migration. Hennepin Island will be managed in a manner that demonstrates scientifically proven techniques in

Figure 3: Location of Mille Lacs NWR [1]

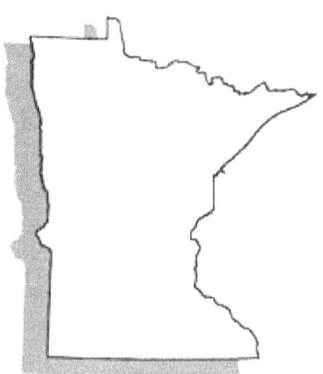

Hennepin Island

*MILLE LACS NATIONAL
WILDLIFE REFUGE*

Spirit Island

*MILLE LACS NATIONAL
WILDLIFE REFUGE*

Mille Lacs Band of Ojibwe Reservation

1.*Source: Department of Natural Resources, Mille Lacs Band of Ojibwe, 2007.*

Sunflowers. USFWS

Common Tern production while Spirit Island will be managed in a way that balances the needs of colonial nesting birds. Management will be in cooperation with the Mille Lacs Band and Minnesota DNR.

Refuge Goals

Considering the purposes of the refuges and our vision for the future, we have established the following goals for Rice Lake NWR and Mille Lacs NWR.

Rice Lake National Wildlife Refuge

Habitat

The Refuge will contain a diversity of habitats typical of historical north-central Minnesota.

Wildlife

Fish and migrating and resident wildlife populations on the Refuge will be naturally diverse, healthy, and self sustaining.

Wildlife-dependent Recreation

Visitors will enjoy wildlife-dependent recreation and they, along with residents of the local community, will appreciate the value and need for fish and wildlife conservation.

Cultural Values

The American Indian community and the Refuge will preserve American Indian cultural values through communication, consultation, and cooperation.

Administration and Operations

Funding, staffing, facilities, and public support will be sufficient to accomplish the purposes, vision, goals, and objectives of the Refuge.

Mille Lacs National Wildlife Refuge

Wildlife

An optimum nesting population of Common Terns will exist on Hennepin Island and we will know the productivity and chronology of species using Spirit Island.

Purpose of the Plan

This CCP describes the management direction for Rice Lake NWR and Mille Lacs NWR for the next 15 years. The refuge manager and staff will use the plan as a reference document when developing work plans and making management decisions. The plan provides guidance and rationale for our management direction.

The plan enhances the management of the Refuges by:

- Providing a clear statement of desired conditions.

- Ensuring management is consistent with laws, policies, and plans.

- Ensuring consideration of preservation of historic properties is part of Refuge management and planning.

- Giving Refuge neighbors, visitors, and the general public an understanding of the Service's management actions on and around the Refuges.

- Establishing continuity in Refuge management.

- Providing a sound basis for budget requests.

Chapter 2: The Planning Process

Meetings and Involvement

The planning process for this CCP began in December 2004. Initially, members of the regional planning staff and Rice Lake NWR staff identified a list of issues and concerns that were associated with the management of the Refuge. These preliminary issues and concerns were based on staff knowledge of the area and contacts with citizens in the community. Refuge staff and Service planners then asked Refuge neighbors, organizations, local government units, and interested citizens to share their thoughts in three open houses.

In April 2005, the public was invited to open houses conducted at the Refuge Visitor Center, the Mille Lacs Band of Ojibwe District 2 East Lake Community Center, which is located one-quarter mile north of the Refuge Headquarters, and at the Mille Lacs Band of Ojibwe Tribal Government Center in Onamia. People were invited through articles in the local papers and individual letters to the members of the East Lake Community. Seventeen people attended the open house at the Visitor Center. Three people attended in Onamia, and seven people came to the East Lake Community Center. People were asked to provide written comments within 30 days. Twenty-six written comments were received during the comment period.

Following the public comment period, an additional meeting was held in the Fish and Wildlife Service Regional Office to review the public comments and identify concerns from subject specialists.

Entrance Sign, Rice Lake NWR. USFWS

Issues

Issues play an important role in planning. Issues focus the planning effort on the most important topics and provide a base for considering alternative approaches to management and evaluating the consequences of managing under these alternative approaches. The issues and concerns expressed during the first phase of planning have been organized under the following headings.

Rice Lake NWR

Management of Rice Lake

Rice Lake is an important area for migrating waterfowl in the fall. Ojibwe Indians have a long tradition of harvesting rice on the lake and will continue harvesting wild rice into the future, as is established by way of an official agreement. There is less rice than in the past and pickerelweed beds are expanding. Since the water control structure was put on the lake, water levels do not vary as much as in the past. We do not have a good understanding of cause and effect of rice management in the lake.

Management of Former Crop Field and Hay Field Areas

There are numerous old field areas on the Refuge that in general are remnants of the pre-refuge farming era. These grassland/brushland areas have been maintained by past management practices of grazing and haying and currently are maintained through prescribed burning. Historically these areas were forested. The largest of these areas is referred to as the old crop fields, located on the southwest end of the Wildlife Drive. The crop fields were cleared and planted to legumes and oats between 1958 and 1962 as part of the Canada Goose reintroduction program. This area was converted to grassland and maintained with haying in the late 1990s through 2002. This grassland area has been maintained with prescribed burning since 2003. Grasslands, and grassland-dependent birds, are greatly diminished within their historic range. However, the Refuge grassland/brushland areas are only minimally successful for high priority breeding grassland birds due to their small acreages and negative edge effects (mammalian predators prefer to hunt along the edges and increased nest parasitism by brown-headed cowbirds). Maintaining the fields as open grassland sites provides wildlife viewing opportunities popular with visitors. Converting all of the old fields to forest would contribute to a large block of unfragmented forest and benefit high priority forest bird species.

Management of Forests

The Refuge lands were forest historically. A large block of diverse forest will benefit bird species that are a high priority for the Service. However, details of how to manage forest to meet biological goals have not been specified.

Wilderness Recommendation

In 1973, a 1,400-acre unit and the 6.27-acre island in Rice Lake were recommended for further consideration by the Secretary of Interior for Wilderness designation. The recommended areas have been managed as de facto wilderness. The Service and the Department have taken no action on the recommendation. The proposed Wilderness does not meet minimum wilderness standards for size (at least 5,000 acres of land or of sufficient size as to make

Fox Sparrow. U.S. Fish & Wildlife Service

practicable its preservation and use in an unimpaired condition). The Wilderness recommendation precludes some management activities.

Indian Community Activities

Ojibwe Indians have a long history of use on the land and harvesting wild rice is important to the Indian community. An easement permits an Indian cemetery on the Refuge. Indian ceremonies are held on the Refuge under special use permit. Some members of the local Indian community desire more facilities and ceremonial opportunities and agreements in perpetuity. Some members also desire unrestricted/unlicensed use of Refuge resources. There are long-term concerns about the cultural impacts caused by Refuge buildings on Indian Point.

Cultural Resources

The Refuge includes pre-historic and historic resources of recognized importance. One view is that interpreting these resources will bring understanding, appreciation, and improved protection of them. Another view is that interpreting resources will make them more broadly known and vulnerable to destruction. In addition, some people would like the recent Indian history of the area interpreted. As a pre-eminent conservation agency, the Service has a responsibility for the protection of the many known and unknown cultural resources located on Refuge lands. Members of the Ojibwe Tribe have requested that the Service remove all buildings from Indian Point, which includes two residences and all of the Refuge maintenance facilities. Indian Point contains the most significant cultural resources known to occur on the Refuge.

Wildlife-dependent Recreation

The National Wildlife Refuge System Improvement Act of 1997 directs refuges to facilitate wildlife-dependent recreation. There may be the opportunity to increase hunting opportunities, although the demand has not been great. Visitors want to see more wildlife on the Refuge and want more wildlife observation opportunities. The public has requested educational programs both on and off the Refuge, and they would like staff available on weekends, or at least Saturdays. There is an unrealized potential in interpretation and environmental education. There is no law enforcement presence on Rice Lake NWR, which raises a concern for visitor safety. The support for wildlife-dependent recreation is presently maximized under current staff and budget.

Sandstone Unit

Operation

Monitoring activities on the Unit are difficult because of its distance from the office. Access within the Unit is difficult because of damage to roads and bisection of the Unit by the Kettle River. Habitat management and law enforcement on the Unit are below Service standards.

Mille Lacs NWR

Common Tern Management

The emphasis of management on Hennepin Island is for the nesting colony of Common Terns, a State-listed threatened species. The nesting substrate of gravel is not reliably present because of changing water levels and erosion by waves. Gulls compete for nesting space on the island and reduce tern nesting success. For that reason, a gull deterrent program that was first implemented in 1993 is in place and includes destruction of gull eggs and placement of an aboveground string grid over the southern one-third of the island to prevent gulls from landing/nesting. This strategy has had positive results.

Preparation of the CCP

The CCP for Rice Lake and Mille Lacs NWRs was prepared by a team consisting of Refuge and Regional Office staff. The CCP was published in two phases and in accordance with the National Environmental Policy Act (NEPA). The Draft Environmental Assessment, published as Appendix A in the Draft CCP, presented two alternatives for future management and identified a preferred alternative.

The Draft CCP/EA was released for public review and comment on June 25, 2007. A Draft CCP/EA or a summary of the document was sent to more than 250 individuals, organizations, and local, state, and federal agencies and elected officials. An open house was held on July 10, 2007, at the Rice Lake NWR Headquarters following release of the draft document. Five people attended the open house. We received a total of 15 comment letters and e-mails during the 30-day review period. Appendix K of the CCP summarizes these comments and our responses.

The preferred alternative was selected and has become the basis of the Final CCP, which will guide management over the next 15 years. It will guide the development of more detailed step-down management plans for specific resource areas and it will underpin the annual budgeting process through submissions to the Refuge Operating Needs System (RONS) and Maintenance Management System (MMS). Most importantly, the CCP lays out the general approach to managing habitat, wildlife, and people at Rice Lake and Mille Lacs National Wildlife Refuges that will direct day-to-day decision-making and actions.

Chapter 3: Refuge Environment

Area Description

Ecological Context

Glaciers formed the major landscape features that we see today on the Refuges. Those features and climate are dominant determinants of the past vegetation of the area. In order to generalize and understand the fundamental aspects of the landscape, scientists have classified areas with similar geological, soil and climatic characteristics. In the Ecological Land Classification for Minnesota, the northwestern portion of Rice Lake NWR lies in the Tamarack Lowlands subsection, which is generally characterized by rolling to flat lake plains, beach ridges and ground moraines. The potential vegetation for this area is black spruce bog, white cedar-tamarack swamp, and aspen-birch forest. The rest of Rice Lake NWR lies in the St. Louis Moraines subsection, characterized by glacial moraines, rolling hills and small short rivers and large lakes. The potential vegetation for the area is aspen-birch forest, and Northern hardwood forest. Mille Lacs NWR and the Sandstone Unit lie in the Mille Lacs Uplands subsection, which is generally characterized by an ice-molded landscape with irregular ground moraines. The potential vegetation for the area is white pine-oak forest, white pine-red pine forest, and cedar-tamarack swamp.

Francis Marschner (1882-1966) mapped the presettlement vegetation of Minnesota based on Public Land Survey notes and landscape patterns. His maps provide a more detailed approximation of the vegetation in the area of Rice Lake NWR prior to European settlement. The reader should use caution in interpreting too much detail into the historic vegetation maps because of the scale and base data that Marschner used. Marschner's interpretation

Twin Lakes, Rice Lake NWR

for the area that is now Rice Lake NWR included the following major habitat categories: aspen-birch, big woods, conifer bogs and swamps, lake, white and red pine and prairie. Maps showing the historic vegetation of Rice Lake NWR and the Sandstone Unit as interpreted from Marschner's map are displayed in Figure 4 and Figure 5.

Socioeconomic Context

The population of Aitkin County in 2000 was 15,301 people. The Minnesota state demographer projects that the county population will grow to 20,370 in 2015 and 22,160 in 2020. In 2000, approximately 2,800 residents were of school age (5 to 19 years). The estimate for school age residents for 2020 is about 3,300. The county is sparsely populated with 8.4 persons per square mile. The average for Minnesota is 61.8 persons per square mile. The ethnic mix for the county's population is 96.4 percent white, 0.2 percent black or African American, 2.3 percent American Indian, 0.6 percent Hispanic or Latino origin, and 0.2 percent Asian. The percent of persons age 5 years or older who speak a lan-

Figure 4: Historic Vegetation, Rice Lake NWR

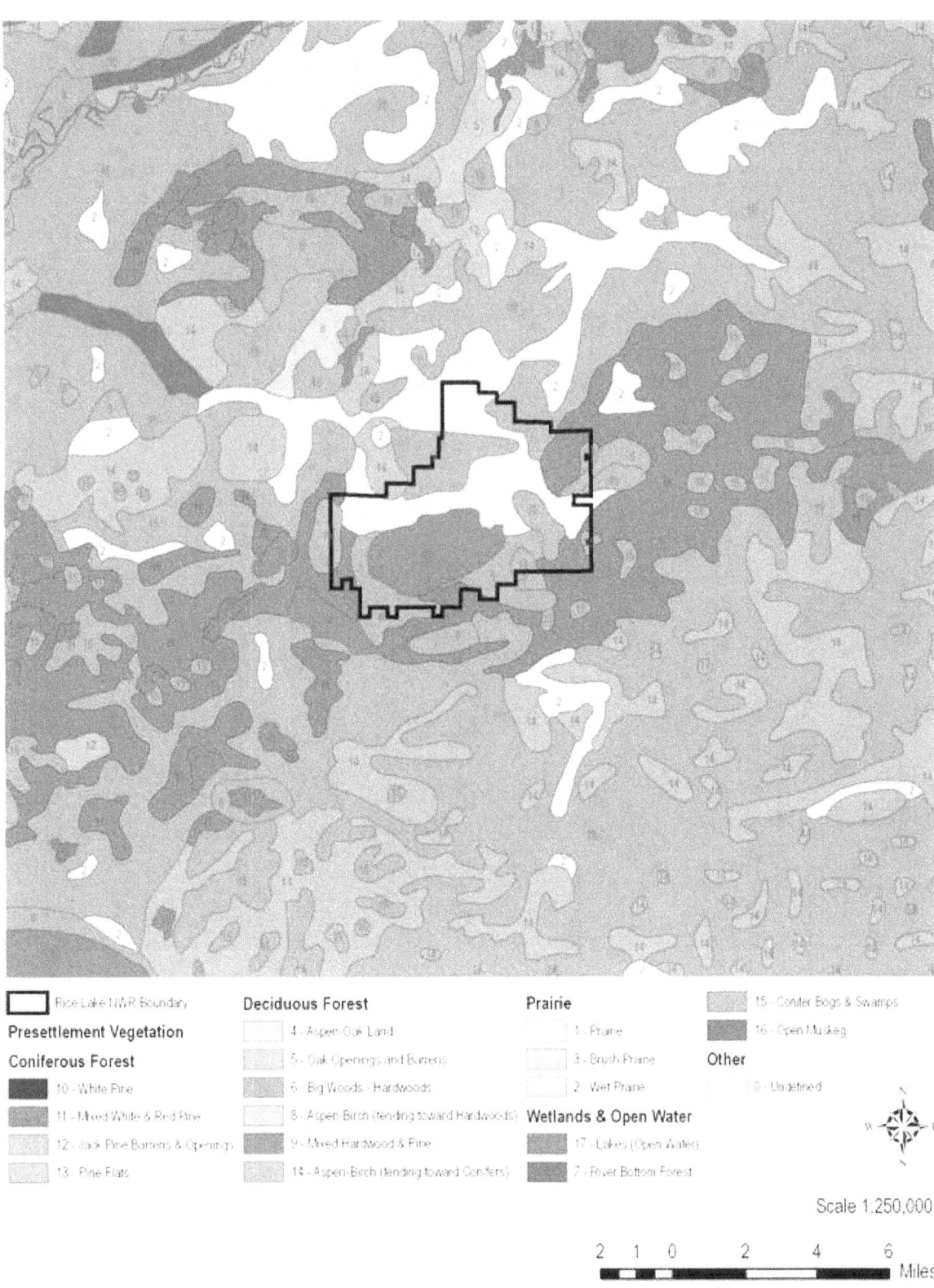

Figure 5: Historical Vegetation, Sandstone Unit of Rice Lake NWR

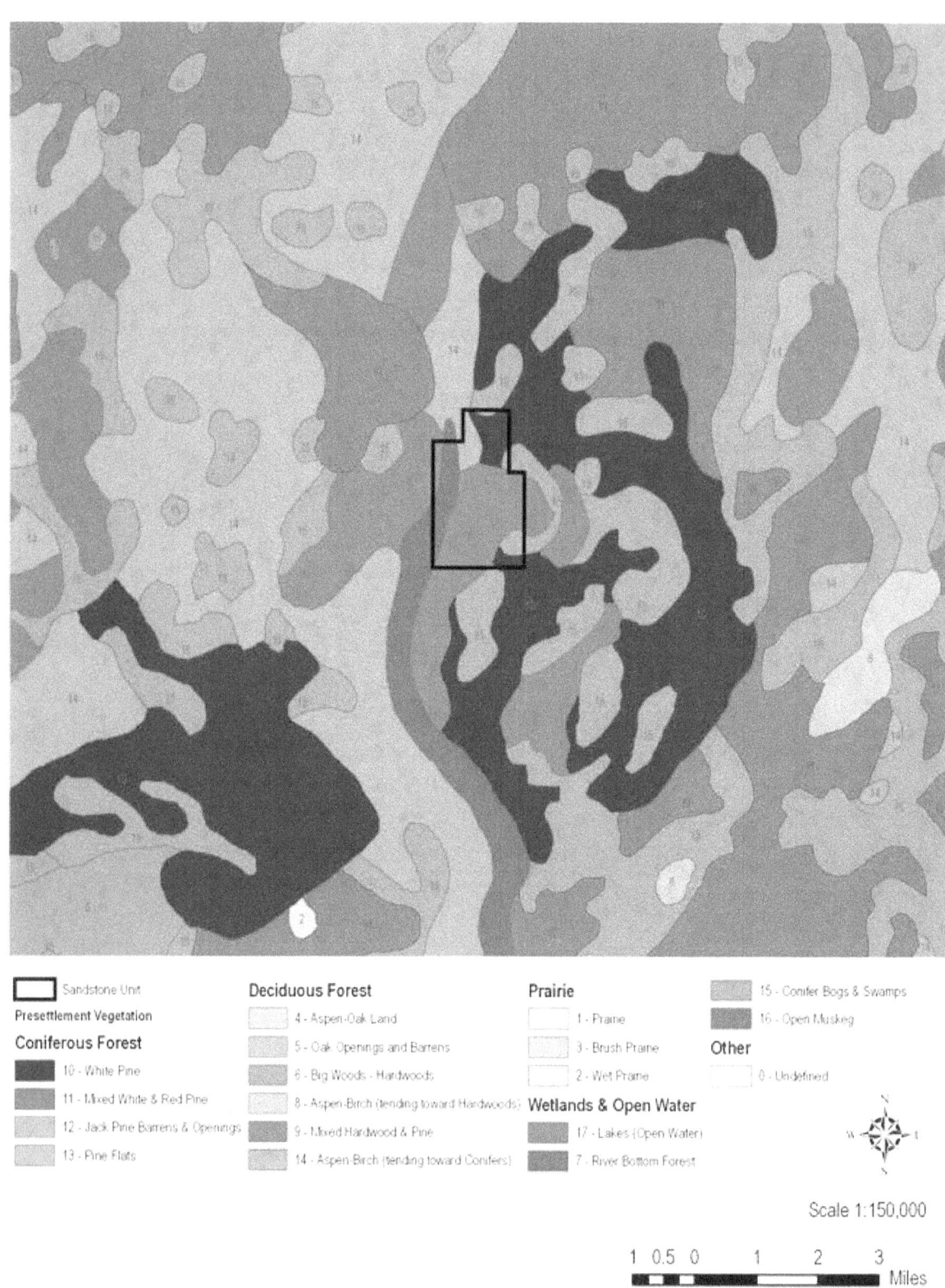

Sandstone Unit

Presettlement Vegetation

Coniferous Forest
10 - White Pine
11 - Mixed White & Red Pine
12 - Jack Pine Barrens & Openings
13 - Pine Flats

Deciduous Forest
4 - Aspen-Oak Land
5 - Oak Openings and Barrens
6 - Big Woods - Hardwoods
8 - Aspen-Birch (tending toward Hardwoods)
9 - Mixed Hardwood & Pine
14 - Aspen-Birch (tending toward Conifers)

Prairie
1 - Prairie
3 - Brush Prairie
2 - Wet Prairie

Wetlands & Open Water
17 - Lakes (Open Water)
7 - River Bottom Forest

15 - Conifer Bogs & Swamps
16 - Open Muskeg

Other
0 - Undefined

Scale 1:150,000

1 0.5 0   1   2   3
Miles

Bobcat, U.S. Fish & Wildlife Service

guage other than English in their home is 3.5 percent. Past population growth is attributed to the creation of new manufacturing jobs and immigration of retirees.

As reported in the 2000 County Business Patterns, Aitkin County had 3,192 employees. The largest employment sectors for the county were health care and social assistance (582), retail trade (569), accommodation and food services (511), manufacturing (479), construction (226), and wholesale trade (192).

"Northeastern Minnesota has traditionally lagged behind the state in terms of income and Aitkin County historically has the lowest income level within the region. Despite diversification of the regional and local economy this situation remains unchanged." (Aitkin County Land Management Plan).

Personal income per capita in 2000 was $20,242 for the county and $31,935 for the state. The median household income was $31,139 for the county and $47,111 for the state. The average earnings per job was $18,375 for the county and $34,836 for the state. The percent of persons below poverty in 1999 was 11.6 percent for the county and 7.9 percent for the state.

Compared to the state, the residents of Aitkin County have less formal education. The percent of persons age 25 or greater who are high school graduates is 80.4 percent for the county and 87.9 percent for the state. The percent of persons age 25 or greater with a bachelor's degree or higher is 11.3 percent for the county and 27.4 percent for the state.

"Tourism is a growing sector of the local economy, and is reflected by the number of second homes located on Big Sandy and northern Mille Lacs Lakes. Snowmobiling and hunting opportunities also draw significant numbers of tourist dollars to the county. Tourism and population growth has implications for the Aitkin County land base, particularly for public lands." "The in-migration of retirees, along with increasing numbers of second home developments, are leading to forestland fragmentation on private lands." (SmartWood, 2004).

Historical Context

Pre-Historical

The earliest evidence of inhabitation by humans is dated to the Woodland Tradition (ca. 500 B.C. – A.D. 1650), which is characterized by the initial appearance of ceramic vessels and the construction of earthen mounds primarily by the Dakota (Sioux) people. In 1897, Jacob Brower and Edward Bromley first mapped the mounds present on what is now the Rice Lake NWR and labeled it the "Bromley Lake Mounds" (Brower 1910). Brower located and mapped 186 mounds in the area extending from the Civilian Conservation Corps (CCC) Camp east to the Indian Point. It is estimated that 114 (61 percent) of those mounds have been destroyed, while 72 (39 percent) remain intact or partially intact. (Johnson, 1990). A subset of the original "Bromley Lake Mounds," presently known as the Mandy Lake Mound Group, contains burial mounds in three forms: 27 are linear, 22 are conical, and six are oval. The distribution or clustering of these varied forms is not random and it is probable that the total group represents mound construction by different socio/cultural groups over a considerable period of time. (Johnson 1990). The Mandy Lake Group is virtually intact and, when combined with the Indian Point mound group, they form one of the largest extant groups of mounds remaining in Minnesota, and certainly contain the largest number of linear mounds in one area. (Johnson 1990). It is believed that these people were nomadic and visited Rice Lake to collect maple syrup and harvest wild rice.

Historical

At the time of Brower and Bromley's visit in 1897, Ojibwe (Chippewa) Indians were present on the landscape. An Ojibwe village and the East Lake Cemetery were located on Indian Point. Sam Yankee and John Aubit (Aubid) were the first Ojibwe to have a warranty of deed dated 1904 on the Indian

Point. By the 1920s, a village consisting of 20-25 Ojibwe families developed around Rice Lake (Ollendorf, 2000). These families lived year-round on the land, harvesting rice and maple syrup, planting gardens and raising some livestock. In the fall, Ojibwe from around the region would travel by foot and horse to gather on the shores of Rice Lake and set up temporary ricing camps. Rice Lake has the distinction of having had one of the last existing ricing camps in the state, if not in the whole wild rice belt. The convenience of the automobile and building of road accesses to chief ricing waters made it unnecessary to camp overnight at ricing sites. Indians at both Rice Lake and Kettle Lake cited the automobile as a cause for the disappearance of camps (Jarvenpa, 1971). Today, members of the Ojibwe people harvest rice in accordance with the Collier Agreement (Appendix G) signed in 1935. Each spring a no fee Special Use Permit (SUP) is issued that allows them to collect maple syrup. The SUP allows them to collect syrup in a limited manner and location as a means to provide traditional education/instruction to Ojibwe youth. They also use the Indian cemetery and hold drumming ceremonies on a sacred area of the Indian Point. No other tribal activities are regularly conducted as the Refuge lies within the Treaty of 1855, which does not reserve the right to hunt, fish or gather on the lands or waters that were ceded.

Besides the fur trade, the first large European influence on the landscape came with the logging industry, which was present around Rice Lake from the 1850s until 1911. Timber (initially white pine) was cut from around Rice Lake in the winter and the logs were skidded to the lake, tied into rafts and floated to the Mississippi River, 20 miles to the west, upon ice-out. In 1897, the American Grass and Twine Company purchased a block of land that is now the portion of Refuge north of the Rice River. They later became known as the Crex Carpet Company and harvested the marsh grass to manufacture carpets until they declared bankruptcy in 1936. In 1900, Davidson and McRae purchased several thousand acres around Rice Lake that they used for ranching until 1917. They were the first to attempt to drain Rice Lake with a hand-dug ditch, which failed to function. They then sold their interests to the St. Croix Land and Lumber Company of Stillwater, Minnesota, which built a sawmill on "Tom's Island," located near the junction of the Wildlife Drive and the South Trail (Johnson, 1945).

In 1910, a branch of the Soo Line Railroad known as the Cuyuna and Iron Range was completed and forms much of what is now the Wildlife Drive. The branch was abandoned in the 1920s. The following years were a mixture of failed farming attempts, market hunting and "guided" duck hunts on the lake. The drought years of the early 1930s and the Great Depression left most of the inhabitants of the area without income and unable to pay their taxes. Much land went into tax-forfeiture and in 1935 was purchased by the U.S. Bureau of Biological Survey to create a migratory waterfowl refuge.

Civilian Conservation Corps (CCC) Camp BS-3, Company 2705, a 23-building camp, was erected on the Refuge and was active from 1939 until 1941. While no buildings remain, the site is clearly marked and identified with an onsite interpretive kiosk and as site number 10 in the Refuge's auto tour brochure. The mission of Company 2705 was the initial development of this land as a federal migratory waterfowl refuge. One of the first projects was to remove rail and ties from the old railroad grade that is now the main refuge road to Highway 65.

Associated Plans and Initiatives

Bird Conservation Initiatives

Several migratory bird conservation plans have been published over the last decade that can be used to help guide management decisions for the Refuge. Bird conservation planning efforts have evolved from a largely local, site-based orientation to a more regional, even inter-continental, landscape-oriented perspective. Several transnational migratory bird conservation initiatives have emerged to help guide the planning and implementation process. The regional plans relevant to Rice Lake and Mille Lacs NWRs are:

- The Upper Mississippi River/Great Lakes Joint Venture Implementation Plan of the North American Waterfowl Management Plan;
- The Partners in Flight Boreal Hardwood Transition [land] Bird Conservation Plan;
- The Upper Mississippi Valley/Great Lakes Regional Shorebird Conservation Plan; and
- The Upper Mississippi Valley/Great Lakes Regional Waterbird Conservation Plan.

Each of the bird conservation initiatives has a process for designating priority species, modeled to a large extent on the Partners in Flight method of computing scores based on independent assessments of global relative abundance, breeding and wintering distribution, vulnerability to threats, area importance, and population trend. These scores are often used by agencies in developing lists of priority bird species. The Service based its 2001 list of Nongame Birds of Conservation Concern primarily on the Partners in Flight, shorebird, and waterbird status assessment scores. Recently, the Minnesota Bird Conservation Initiative (MBCI) has been established by federal and state agencies and statewide conservation organizations. The MBCI will integrate all bird conservation plans and step them down to a local level. This will allow Rice Lake and Mille Lacs NWRs to better refine population and habitat objectives and determine the role it should play in regional bird conservation.

Minnesota Comprehensive Wildlife Conservation Strategy

In 2005, Minnesota completed the Comprehensive Wildlife Conservation Strategy (CWCS), a strategic plan to better manage populations of "species in greatest conservation need" in Minnesota. The plan was developed with the support of funding from the State Wildlife Grant Program created by Congress in 2001. The heart of the strategic plan is for a partnership of conservation organizations across Minnesota to work together to sustain the populations of the identified species. Members of the partnership include the Minnesota Department of Natural Resources, the U.S. Fish and Wildlife Service, The Nature Conservancy, Audubon Minnesota, and the University of Minnesota, as well as many other agencies and conservation organizations. The plan outlines priority conservation actions that might be undertaken by partners.

The organizational units of the CWCS are 25 ecological subsections within Minnesota. Rice Lake and Mille Lacs NWRs occur within the Tamarack Lowlands, St. Louis Moraines, and Mille Lacs Uplands subsections. (Figure 6) The information and strategies of the CWCS were used as a means to assist with development of Refuge objectives in the CCP. The townships that enclose Rice Lake NWR have been identified as containing the highest abundance of species of greatest conservation need within the St. Louis Moraines and Tamarack Lowlands subsections, which suggests that the Refuge plays a key role in the state's conservation partnership. Appendix C of Minnesota's CWCS contains a summary of other conservation plans and efforts for each subsection.

Climate

The Refuge experiences long, cold winters and cool summers. The average annual rainfall, which mostly comes during the spring and fall, is about 27 inches. Snowfall averages about 60 inches per year. The temperature extremes for the year can range from minus-40 degrees Fahrenheit to 100 degrees Fahrenheit. Lakes typically freeze over in early-November and remain frozen until mid-to-late-April. The growing season, the time between the last frost in the spring and the first frost in the fall, is about 118 days.

Geology and Soils

The dominate Refuge surface features were formed by glaciers over 10,000 years ago. A system of moraines, or glacial ridges, in the shape of a huge horseshoe surrounds the area on three sides with the open end to the northeast. One set of ridges formed Rice Lake itself. Scattered islands and glacial ridges rise above the surrounding bog and are covered with timber and other upland plants. Glacial material consisting of rocks, gravel, sand, and clay covers the area's bedrock in layers ranging from 50 to 300 feet thick.

Water and Hydrology

Rice Lake NWR is bisected by the Rice River, which drains the Refuge, flowing from the southeast corner to the northwest, and empties into the Mississippi River 20 miles to the west. The land's natural water drainage toward the south has been blocked by the moraines. This wet area is slowly filling in with sediment and vegetation, becoming a floating or muskeg-like bog.

The Sandstone Unit is crossed by several small streams, flowing east to west to join the Kettle River. The Kettle River, which flows through the western portion of the Unit, has cut a steep sided canyon approximately 100 feet deep and 3,000 to 4,000 feet wide. This portion of the Kettle River is a part of the State of Minnesota Wild and Scenic River System.

Mille Lacs NWR is located approximately 1 mile from any shoreline of Mille Lacs Lake. The water

Figure 6: Minnesota Comprehensive Wildlife Conservation Strategy Units, Rice Lake NWR

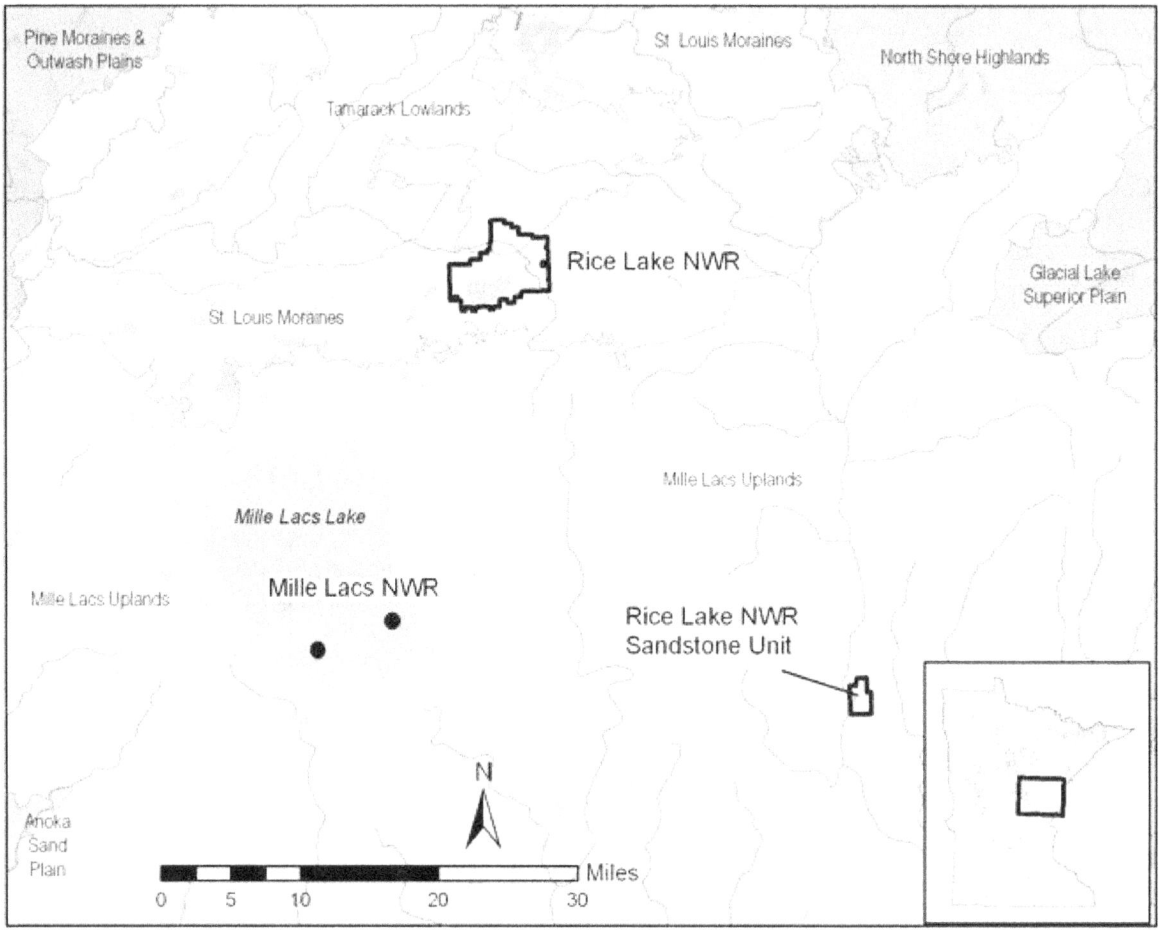

level in Mille Lacs Lake affects the size of the islands and their vulnerability to erosion by wave action. Seiches occur on the lake and account for brief, but record changes in water levels. A seiche can be described as a large wave or storm surge that is created by dramatic changes in atmospheric pressure coupled with high winds. The effects of a seiche to nesting Common Terns on this low lying island can be devastating. The more persistent changes in water level are influenced by broader weather patterns. Over the last 10 years the water level has had a range of about 3 feet. Figure 7 displays the water level data for Mille Lacs Lake for the last 10 years (Minnesota Department of Natural Resources).

Refuge Resources

The wild rice wetlands on Rice Lake NWR and the relationship between wild rice and Ring-necked Ducks are of vital importance and need to be highlighted. Tyically during the second and third weeks of October, over 100,000 Ring-necked Ducks will be feeding and resting on the wild rice beds in Rice Lake. A noteworthy exception occurred during the second week of October 1994, when more than 1 million ducks were observed, of which 60 percent were Ring-necked Ducks and 40 percent were Mallards, a Minnesota record for the most waterfowl observed in one location at one time (Lapp 1995).

Wild rice is high in protein and vitamins and helps waterfowl recover quickly from the demands of migration. Ten to 15 percent of a duck's body weight is lost during a day dominated by flight. If

Figure 7: Lake Mille Lacs Water Levels, 1995-2005

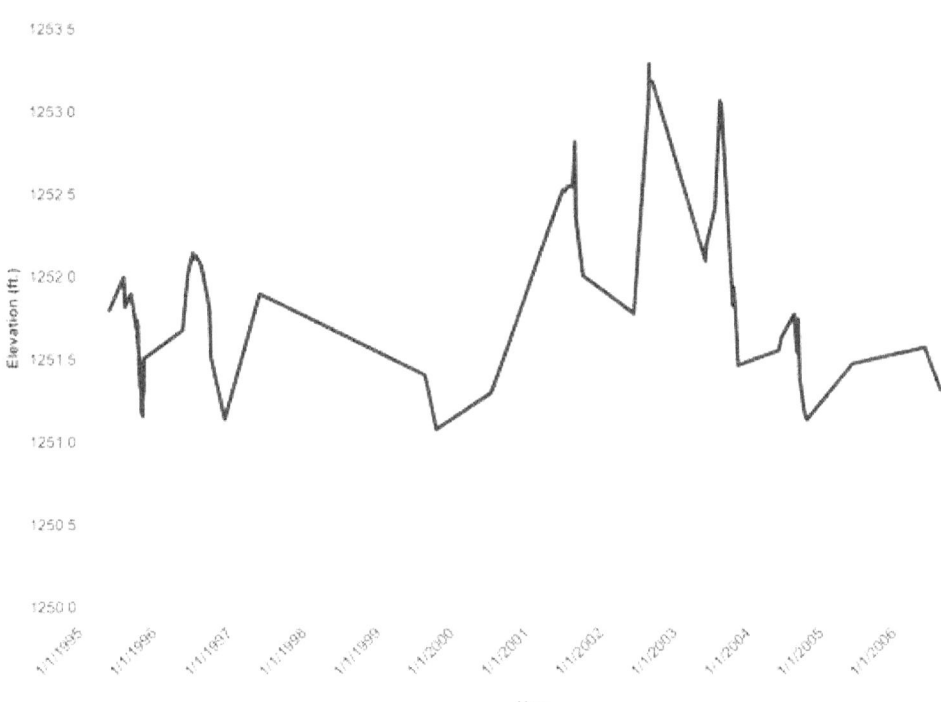

those birds have adequate habitat, good food resources and little disturbance they can rebound in just 1 to 3 days (Norrgard 2005). A suite of wetland birds also nest and feed in Refuge wild rice beds during the summer. Examples of rare and declining species, and/or the Services' Region 3 Resource Conservation Priority Species that use wild rice habitat include:

- Common Loon
- American Bittern
- Trumpeter Swan
- Bald Eagle
- Northern Harrier
- Yellow Rail
- Greater Yellowlegs
- Marbled Godwit
- Stilt Sandpiper
- Black Tern

Common Loons and American Bitterns nest along the undisturbed shores. Trumpeter Swans are once again nesting and raising broods in lakes where they have been absent for many years. Bald Eagles nest in the nearby forest and feed on the fish and waterfowl that are associated with wild rice

lakes. Northern Harriers nest and hunt in the marsh edge. Yellow Rails nest in the lake's emergergent plant zones. Greater Yellow-legs, Marbled Godwit, Stilt Sandpiper, and other shorebird species feed on invertebrates in the wild rice straw mats and in the mudflats during their spring and fall migration. Black Terns use the wild rice straw mats as nesting platforms. Other wildlife species that commonly feed on wild rice include ducks, geese Sora, American Coot, blackbirds, deer beaver, and muskrats. Blackbirds and warblers are drawn to the invertebrate prey found in wild rice habitat while marshbirds feed on the small vertebrate species found there.

American Indian cultures throughout the northern Midwest and northeast have traditionally harvested wild rice. Such activities are supported by the Refuge System and allow American Indians contact with their culture as well as providing a source of income.

The range of wild rice has contracted greatly since European settlement. The boom and bust ecology of wild rice creates highly fluctuating annual production cycles. Some of the causal factors of this oscillation are the buildup of rice straw from the previous year's growth, sediment nutrient levels and water depth. By preserving/restoring healthy wild rice beds we are preserving healthy wetland habitat for the benefit of many species, including our own.

Plant Communities

Forest

Rice Lake NWR lies within the transition zone between the coniferous forests of Northern Minnesota and the deciduous hardwood forests typical of the southern portion of the state. Historically, white pine was very abundant in the pre-settlement mixed forests of the region, but logging in the late 1800s resulted in replacement of pine with quaking aspen, red and sugar maples, paper birch, basswood, and red oak. Today there are approximately 4,222 acres of upland forest on the Refuge (lowland or submontane cold-deciduous forest per the National Vegetation Classification System, NVCS). Lowland forest stands are characterized by tamarack, black spruce, black ash, balsam fir, and white cedar. There are approximately 3,259 acres of lowland forest on the Refuge (temporarily flooded cold-deciduous forest and saturated cold-deciduous forest, NVCS). See Figure 8.

Brushland is a difficult habitat type to classify. Brushland typically occurs in areas that were once farmed, grazed or hayed and have been left undisturbed for years, allowing brush to invade the grassland. In some systems, the bog areas are classified as brushland due to the expanses of invading brush species found dominating the native sedge species. In the case of the Refuge, brush is considered an undesirable condition, hence, brush-dominated areas will be discussed as acreages in their desired condition of forest, bog or grassland.

Rice Lake NWR also includes a Research Natural Area that consists of 100 acres of tamarack located between Rice Lake and the Rice River.

The Sandstone Unit consists of approximately 1,315 acres of upland forest (Figure 9). The terrain is gently rolling to nearly flat. The presettlement vegetation was primarily pine, maple, oak and tamarack. Bearing trees listed in 1849 and 1851 Government Land Office surveys show primarily white pine and tamarack with a few aspen, red oak, maple, jack pine, and spruce. Francis Marschner's map of the Original Vegetation of Minnesota shows vegetation cover in the vicinity of the Sandstone Unit as being white pine groves, mixed hardwood and pine, and conifer bog and swamp. However, like most of the surrounding area, the virgin pine forests were extensively exploited by white settlers. Few examples of this original vegetation are now found anywhere in the county.

Most of the wooded uplands of the Sandstone Unit are now occupied by a relatively even aged (40-60 years) aspen/birch timber type that includes a mature red pine component. Some areas of this aspen/birch type are beginning to succeed to maple/basswood. There is also a 116-acre timber type that is dominated by red pine with an intermediate association of aspen, maple, oak and birch. The understory of the red pine type is hazel brush of medium density. Regeneration is slight to non-existent in part due to deer browsing and lack of disturbance such as fire. This pine type is probably close to what represents the dominant presettlement vegetation for the Unit. The large pines on the Unit apparently became established immediately following the "Great Hinckley Fire" of 1894.

Bog

Rice Lake NWR bog lands are classified as saturated temperate or subpolar grasslands in the NVCS. There are approximately 5,791 acres of this habitat type on the Refuge. The bogs are flat expanses of poorly drained organic soils known as peat. They support a dense, spongy mixture of flowering plants, grasses, low shrubs, and small stands of black spruce, balsam fir and tamarack. Shallow lakes with marshy shorelines dot this landscape. Peat is formed from successive layers of partly decomposed vegetable matter, mostly sphagnum moss. The peat makes the bog soil acidic and tints bog waters a clear amber color. A muskeg or floating bog is created in a poorly drained lake that is slowly filling-in with vegetation. Dense collections of floating plants at the lake's margin offer a seedbed for more vegetation. Soon a floating mat forms that builds sediment on the lake bottom, paving the way for other water-tolerant plants and shrubs. A floating bog mat will eventually cover the water's surface and, over a long period of time, turn what was once a lake into a lowland forest.

The greatest expanse of bog on the Refuge is located on the north side of the Refuge. This area surrounds the Rice River and is over 3,000 acres in size. Some classification systems describe this area as a "brushland" though by description it has only achieved an overgrowth of brush due to the lack of a disturbance factor, such as wildfire, over the past 70 years. The native vegetation within the bog would have consisted of sedge species with sporadic areas

Figure 8: Current Landcover, Rice Lake NWR

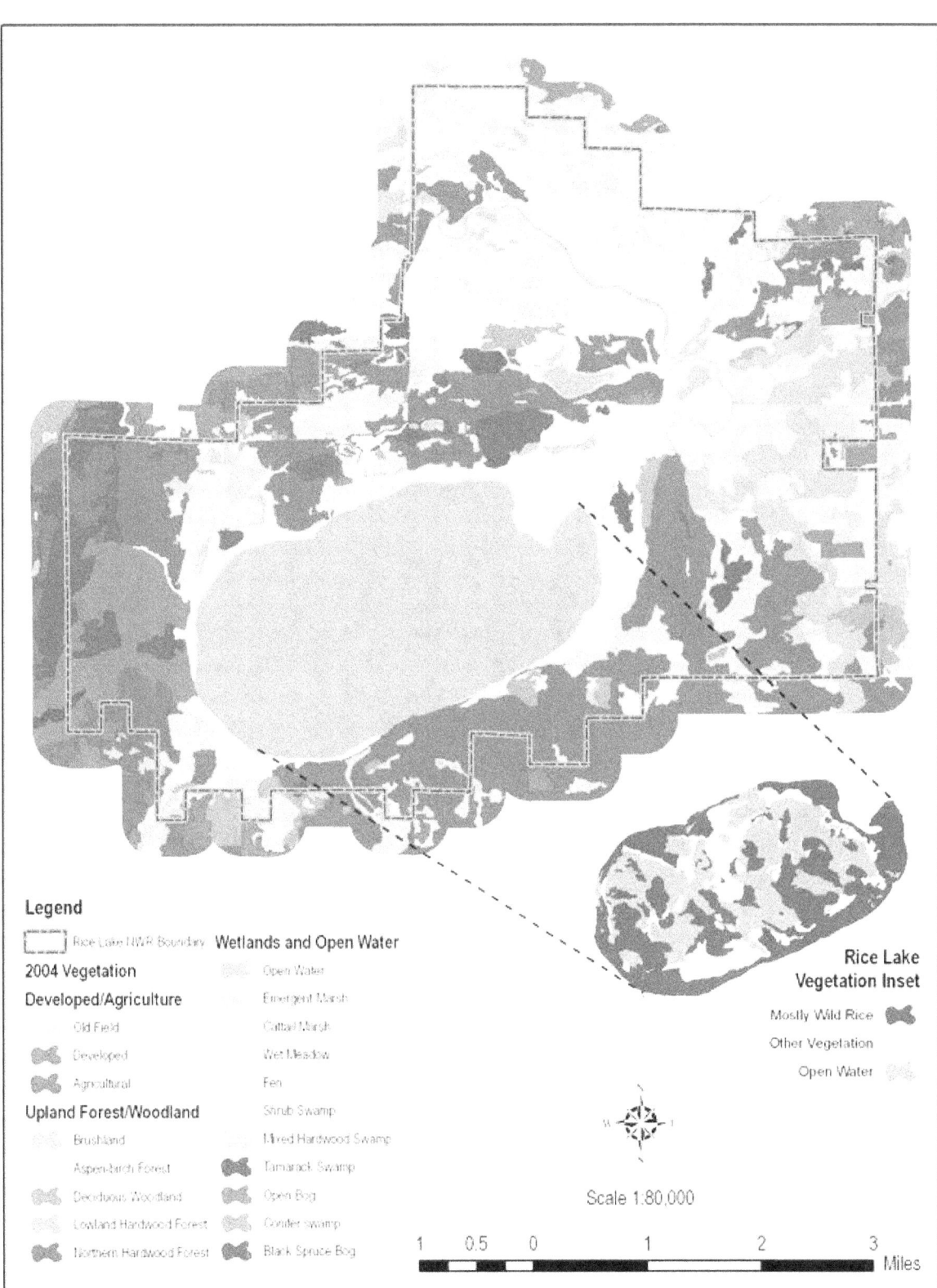

Figure 9: Current Landcover, Sandstone Unit of Rice Lake NWR

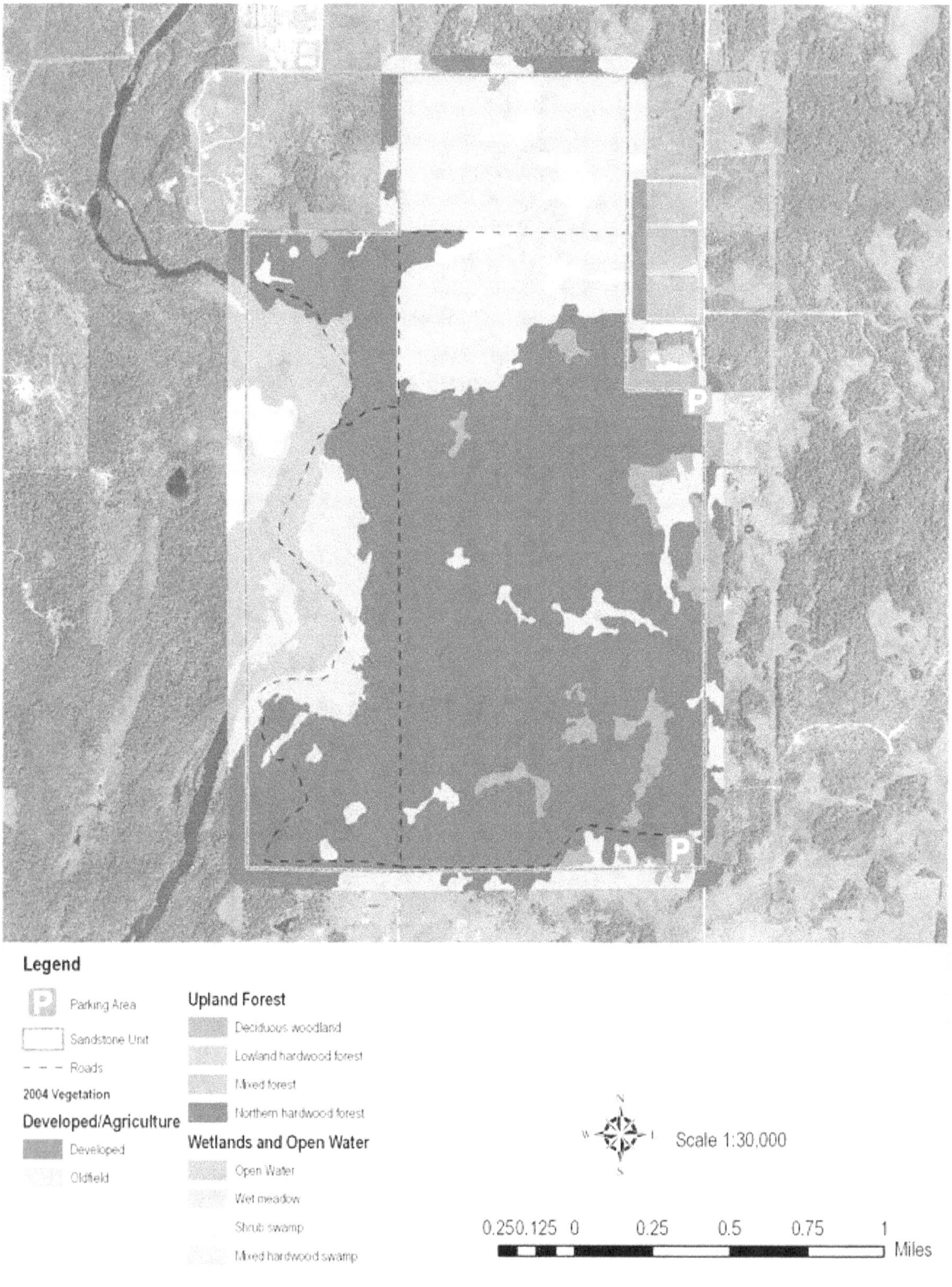

Legend

P Parking Area

☐ Sandstone Unit

– – – Roads

2004 Vegetation

Developed/Agriculture

Developed

Oldfield

Upland Forest

Deciduous woodland

Lowland hardwood forest

Mixed forest

Northern hardwood forest

Wetlands and Open Water

Open Water

Wet meadow

Shrub swamp

Mixed hardwood swamp

Scale 1:30,000

0.25 0.125 0   0.25   0.5   0.75   1
Miles

of brush, like willow and dogwood. Prescribed fire has been the management tool used to decrease and inhibit further brush invasion into this bog.

Grassland

Rice Lake NWR maintains approximately 678 acres of grassland (medium-tall sod temperate or subpolar grassland, NVCS), which were created through the clearing of timber and brush by former landowners and planted to species suitable for hay cutting and grazing. Since 2003, these open areas have been maintained through the use of prescribed burning. The majority of these fields contain non-indigenous species (smooth brome and timothy), although a couple of small fields were planted to tall-grass prairie cultivars (big blue stem, Indian grass) by Refuge staff in the late 1980s. The largest grassland block is 148 acres. It occurs on the west end of the Refuge in the former crop-fields area.

The Sandstone Unit has approximately 406 acres of grass/brushland that exist primarily as a result of previous land clearing activities by the Federal Correctional Institution. The open area on the north end of the Unit was cleared of trees for agricultural development. This area was kept open through haying under a permit system until 2001.

Aquatic

The main body of water on Rice Lake NWR is Rice Lake, which is approximately 3,600 acres, or

Herring Gull on a nest, U.S. Fish & Wildlife Service

nearly one-quarter of the Refuge, and has 9.5 miles of shoreline. Rice Lake is a shallow, natural wild rice producing wetland. Average water depth is 2 feet and the bottom is a composition of mud and silt. Vegetation in the lake is dominated by wild rice and pickerelweed. Although pickerelweed is a native species, it is acting as an invasive in the lake. This dominance has been accentuated by the stable water levels needed to produce wild rice. Other vegetation present in the lake include: bulrush, cattail, wild celery, and a variety of pondweeds. The lake is known as a bigmouth buffalo and northern pike spawning and rearing area. A ditch and water control structure were built on the inlet/outlet to the lake in the early 1950s. A larger capacity structure was completed in 1979.

Other major water bodies on the Refuge include Mandy Lake, Twin Lakes and the Rice River. Mandy Lake is an open body lake with beds of wild rice, cattail, and common reed around the perimeter. The lake is 101 acres and has approximately 2.1 miles of shoreline with a maximum depth of 16 feet. Mandy Lake is connected to the Rice River via a floating bog. During times of high water, it is possible for fish to move under the bog.

Twin Lakes is a classic example of a developing bog. The two lakes have a combined surface area of 16 acres with a maximum depth of 50 feet and 0.6 mile of shoreline. The shoreline is filling-in with peat and vegetation and provides an excellent example of bog succession and contains species like lady-slipper and pitcher plant.

The Rice River traverses the Refuge from the southeast corner to the northwest corner. The river originates in the Solana State Forest, 7 miles south of the Refuge. The river is fed by Porcupine Lake and numerous small tributaries as it flows northwestward into the Refuge. The Refuge receives drainage from approximately 155 square miles of the Rice River watershed. The river averages 70 feet wide and 2.5 feet deep. The river serves as both the inlet and outlet to Rice Lake depending on the flow and water level in the lake. A water control structure (Radial Gates) located on the North Bog Road was installed in 1952 to form the Rice River Pool. During high water times, the Pool will cover 2,500 acres. Sedge mats that support heavy growths of common reed, wild rice, cattail, and willow dominate the pool. Even when the pool is completely flooded, little increase in open water is achieved

Largemouth Bass, U.S. Fish & Wildlife Service

because of a propensity for the mat to float. The open water area of Rice River Pool seldom exceeds 300 acres.

Fish and Wildlife Communities

Birds

A total of 242 species of birds has been confirmed on Rice Lake NWR (Appendix D). Waterfowl, raptors, and songbirds are commonly observed on the Refuge. Rice Lake NWR has been designated a Globally Important Bird Area by the American Bird Conservancy. This designation was granted due to the importance of the lake and its naturally producing wild rice as a food source to migrating waterfowl, especially Ring-necked Ducks. More than 100,000 Ring-necked Ducks are typically found in the wild rice beds on Rice Lake during the second and third weeks of October. In 1994, Ring-necked Ducks numbered 600,000 during a single survey period. The Refuge has also been designated as a State Important Bird Area, as part of the larger McGregor Important Bird Area, by the National Audubon Society.

The two islands that comprise Mille Lacs NWR serve as nesting sites for colonial waterbirds. Hennepin Island is the site of one of four Common Tern breeding colonies in Minnesota. The Common Tern is a Minnesota State Threatened species. Spirit Island has nesting Ring-billed and Herring Gulls, and Double-crested Cormorants. Many species of waterbird, shorebird and waterfowl have also been observed on the islands, including American White Pelicans, Caspian Terns, Dunlin, Red Knots, Ruddy Turnstones, Common and Red-breasted Mergansers and Mallards.

Mammals

Forty-three species of mammals have been confirmed on Rice Lake NWR. (Appendix D). White-

tailed deer, black bear, porcupine, snow-shoe hare, bobcat, beaver, coyote and red fox are commonly observed species on the Refuge. The Refuge is home to at least one pack of gray wolves and Canada lynx have been observed. Though a rare occurrence, moose have also been seen on the Refuge.

Amphibians and Reptiles

Three species of reptiles have been confirmed on Rice Lake NWR. Literature searches indicate that four species could be found on the Refuge. Eight species of amphibians have been documented on the Refuge. Literature searches indicate that 12 species could be present. (Appendix D).

Fish

Fish surveys are conducted by the Minnesota DNR and the Service's Ashland, Wisconsin, Fishery Resource Office (FRO) on a sporadic basis. Sampling by various methods has located 21 species including northern pike, yellow perch, bluegill, black and brown bullheads, bigmouth buffalo, white suckers, bowfin, golden shiner and walleye (Appendix D). The Refuge is best known for spring and fall runs of northern pike in and out of Rice Lake via the Rice River. The Minnesota DNR conducts a "fish rescue" each fall when the dissolved oxygen level falls to a certain level, forcing the northern pike to leave the lake. Fish traps are then placed in the water control structure at Rice Lake to capture the departing northern pike. The pike are transported to lakes primarily around the Twin City metro area. While trapping northern pike may once have been commonplace in Minnesota, DNR officials have said that the trapping effort at Rice Lake NWR is the last such place in the state. The average catch is around 4,000 pounds per year.

Mussels and Clams

A literature search indicates that 13 species of mussels have ranges that include Rice Lake NWR. Surveys have found and identified five species and one unknown species. The surveys were conducted by FRO divers in July 2004. The most common species found during the surveys were the fat mucket (*Lampsilis siliquiodea*); paper pondshell (*Utterbackia imbecillis*); eastern floater (*Pyganodon cataracta* sp.) (pending verification); giant floater (*Pyganodon grandis*); and the strange floater, *Strophitus undulatus*. Fingernail clams (*Sphaeridae* sp.), were also found throughout the Refuge. No mussels were found in Mandy Lake during the survey, possibly because aquatic plant growth was very heavy throughout the shoreline. Four of the five freshwater mussels and clam are common species and found throughout the Midwest. The fifth species, the eastern floater (*Pyganodon cataracta* sp.), a freshwater mussel looking very similar to the giant floater (*Pyganodon grandis*), is not currently listed as being found in Minnesota. Malacologists with the Minnesota DNR are reviewing these two mussels. Funding was secured by the Refuge in early 2006 for comparative DNA analysis to verify the species identity (Appendix D).

Invertebrates

No formalized invertebrate sampling has been conducted on the Refuge. A literature search indicates that 103 species of butterflies and moths and 95 species of dragonfly/damselflies could exist on the Refuge. Freshwater invertebrate samples have been taken for environmental education purposes but not documented (Appendix D).

Threatened and Endangered Species

Federally-listed threatened animal species that have been confirmed on the Refuge include the Bald Eagle and the Canada lynx. State-listed endangered or threatened bird species include the Trumpeter Swan and Henslow's Sparrow. One state-listed bird species, the Common Tern, nests on Mille Lacs NWR. The state-listed plant, triangle moonwort, is found on Rice Lake NWR.

Wildlife Species of Concern

Nearly everyone recognizes that all species are important to a healthy ecosystem. However, over the last few years, members of the conservation community have realized that with limited fiscal resources it is necessary to identify which species should be prioritized. The federal and state lists of threatened and endangered species identify one set of priority species. In the Fish and Wildlife Service's Region 3, representatives of the migratory bird, endangered species, and fisheries programs identified species that require the most attention given our current level of knowledge. Migratory bird conservation initiatives also contribute to setting priorities. The base for Minnesota's Comprehensive Wildlife Conservation Strategy was the identification of the "species of greatest conservation need." The several efforts to identify priority species are highly inter-related with cross-references and the same experts contributing to multiple projects. In general, the species priority reflects population levels that are rare or declining and below levels that

ensure their long-term stability. Region 3 priorities also included species with recreational or economic value and species with a "nuisance" level.

Table 1 summarizes information on wildlife habitat and species relationships for species of management concern for Rice Lake and Mille Lacs National Wildlife Refuges. The species were chosen from the FWS Region 3 January 2002 list of Fish & Wildlife Resource Conservation Priorities. The relationship table is adapted from the "Aitkin County Forest Management Plan," which was based on the Wildlife Habitat Association Database developed for and used on the Chippewa National Forest.

Appendix C compiles the FWS Region 3 Resource Conservation Priorities and the Minnesota list of species of greatest conservation need applicable for Rice Lake and Mille Lacs National Wildlife Refuges.

Threats to Resources

Invasive Species

Rice Lake NWR

Invasive species are considered one of the greatest threats to the National Wildlife Refuge System and Rice Lake NWR. The list of presently known invasive plant species includes common reed, reed canary grass, purple loosestrife, leafy spurge, and European buckthorn. It is probably only a matter of time before such species as Gypsy moth (100 miles distant), emerald ash borer, zebra mussel (40 miles distant), Asian carp, and the New Zealand mud snail (50 miles distant) also appear.

Mille Lacs NWR

Zebra mussels are present in Mille Lacs Lake but are not expected to directly impact Mille Lacs NWR. The potential impacts to the food chain for the avian species that use Mille Lacs NWR, especially the Common Tern population, are of greater concern.

Contaminants

Mercury is a pervasive contaminant across Minnesota, necessitating a statewide Fish Consumption Advisory from the Minnesota Department of Health. Air pollution is the major source of mercury contamination to Minnesota's lakes and rivers. About 70 percent of the mercury in the air is the result of emissions from coal combustion, mining, and the incineration of mercury-containing prod-

Table 1: Wildlife Habitat and Species Relationship for Species of Management Concern, Rice Lake NWR (including the Sandstone Unit) and Mille Lacs NWR

Species	Open Water / River / Wetland								Opening		Forest Habitats													
	Lake	Pond	Stream-River	Emergent Non-Perm Wetland	Emergent Permanent Wetland	Sedge Meadow Wetland	Shrub Sapling Wetland	Open Heath Bog	Permanent Forest Opening	Shrub Sapling Opening	Semi-Open Lowland Conifer	Closed Canopy Lowland	Young Deciduous Upland	Mature Deciduous Upland	Old Deciduous Upland	Young Coniferous Upland	Mature Coniferous Upland	Old Coniferous Upland	Young Mixed Upland	Mature Mixed Upland	Old Mixed upland	Young Lowland Deciduous	Mature Lowland Deciduous	Old Lowland Deciduous
Gray Wolf	f					f	f		x	x		f	x	x	x	x	x	x	x	x	x	x	x	x
American Bittern	f	f	f	f	x	x	f		x	x														
American Woodcock			f	f			f		x	x	x		x						x					
Bald Eagle	f	f	f											b	b		b	b		b	b			
Black Tern	f	f	f	x	x																			
Black-billed Cuckoo	f	f	f	f			x				x								x					
Black-crowned Night Heron	f	f	f	f	f		x				x	x	x	x					x	x				
Blue-winged Teal	f	f	f	f	f	x	f																	
Bobolink						x		x			b													
Buff-breasted Sandpiper	f				f			f																
Canada Goose	x	x	x	x	f																			
Canada Warbler							x	f	x		x	x	x	x					x	x		x	x	
Canvasback	f	f	f	f	f																			
Common Loon	f	f	f	f	f																			
Common Tern	x	f	f	f	x																			
Connecticut Warbler								x	x		x													
Dickcissel									x															
Double-crested Cormorant*	f	f	f	f																				
Eastern Meadowlark									x		x													
Field Sparrow						x		x			x													
Forster's Tern	f				x	f																		
Golden-winged Warbler						x					x	x	f	f										
Grasshopper Sparrow						x		x	x		x													
Greater Yellowlegs	f	f	f	f	f	f																		

Table 1: Wildlife Habitat and Species Relationship for Species of Management Concern, Rice Lake NWR (including the Sandstone Unit) and Mille Lacs NWR

Species	Open Water / River / Wetland								Opening		Forest Habitats													
	Lake	Pond	Stream-River	Emergent Non-Perm Wetland	Emergent Permanent Wetland	Sedge Meadow Wetland	Shrub Sapling Wetland	Open Heath Bog	Permanent Forest Opening	Shrub Sapling Opening	Semi-Open Lowland Conifer	Closed Canopy Lowland	Young Deciduous Upland	Mature Deciduous Upland	Old Deciduous Upland	Young Coniferous Upland	Mature Coniferous Upland	Old Coniferous Upland	Young Mixed Upland	Mature Mixed Upland	Old Mixed upland	Young Lowland Deciduous	Mature Lowland Deciduous	Old Lowland Deciduous
Henslow's Sparrow						x		x			x													
Hudsonian Godwit	f	f		f	f																			
Least Bittern				f	x	x	f																	
LeConte's Sparrow	f	f		f	f	x		x			x													
Lesser Scaup	f	f		f	f	x		f			x													
Long-eared Owl						f		f	f	f	f	f	f	b	b	f	b	b	f	b	b			
Mallard	x	x		f	f	b	b		f	f	b	b	b	b	b	b	b	b	b	b	b			
Marbled Godwit	f	f		f	f																			
Nelson's Sharp-tailed Sparrow						x					f													
Northern Flicker									f		x	x	x	x	x	b	b	b	b	x	b			
Northern Goshawk							x			x	f	x	x	x		f	x	x	b	x	x			
Northern Harrier	f			f		x		x			x	f												
Northern Pintail	f	f		f	f						f													
Olive-sided Flycatcher	f							f	f	f	f		f	f		f	f	f	f		f	x	x	x
Orchard Oriole													f	f			f		f	x				
Peregrine Falcon	f		f		f			f	f		f													
Red-headed Woodpecker							f		f		x	x	x	x	x	b				x			f	x
Red-shouldered Hawk						f	f	f			f	f	b	b	b								b	x
Sedge Wren				x	x	x	x						x									x		
Short-billed Dowitcher	f	f		f	x	f																		
Short-eared Owl			f	f	f	x	f	f			x	f			b									
Snow Goose	f										x													
Stilt Sandpiper	f	f	f	f	f						f													
Trumpeter Swan	x	x	f																					

Table 1: Wildlife Habitat and Species Relationship for Species of Management Concern, Rice Lake NWR (including the Sandstone Unit) and Mille Lacs NWR

Species	Open Water / River / Wetland								Opening		Forest Habitats													
	Lake	Pond	Stream-River	Emergent Non-Perm Wetland	Emergent Permanent Wetland	Sedge Meadow Wetland	Shrub Sapling Wetland	Open Heath Bog	Permanent Forest Opening	Shrub Sapling Opening	Semi-Open Lowland Conifer	Closed Canopy Lowland	Young Deciduous Upland	Mature Deciduous Upland	Old Deciduous Upland	Young Coniferous Upland	Mature Coniferous Upland	Old Coniferous Upland	Young Mixed Upland	Mature Mixed Upland	Old Mixed upland	Young Lowland Deciduous	Mature Lowland Deciduous	Old Lowland Deciduous
Upland Sandpiper											f													
Western Meadowlark											f													
Whimbrel	f	f		f	f			f			f													
Whip-poor-will		f		f	f						f		b	b	b				b	b			f	f
Wilson's Phalarope	f	f		f	f	f																		
Wood Duck	f	f		f	f	f								x	x					x			x	x
Wood Thrush														x	x					x	x		x	x
Yellow Rail					x	x																		
Brook Trout – Inland population			x																					
Lake Sturgeon – Inland population			x																					
American Burying Beetle							x				x		x	x		x	x		x	x		x	x	
Black Sandshell			x																					
Elktoe			x																					
Round Pigtoe			x																					
Snail spp.													x						x			x		
Threeridge			x																					
Zebra Mussel *	x		x		x																			
Rusty Crayfish *	x		x		x																			

b = uses habitat for breeding; f = uses habitat for feeding; x = uses habitat for both breeding and feeding; *"Nuisance" species

Twin Lakes, Rice Lake NWR

ucts, the remaining 30 percent is derived from natural emissions. Only about 10 percent of Minnesota's mercury contamination originates from Minnesota emissions, however 90 percent of Minnesota's emissions are deposited in other states and countries. (Minnesota Pollution Control Agency, 2005). The Kettle River, which flows through the Sandstone Unit, is on the Minnesota Impaired Water list with mercury as the pollutant and includes a specific Fish Consumption Advisory. No other contaminants are known to exist on Rice Lake NWR.

Climate Change Impacts

The U.S. Department of the Interior issued an order in January 2001 requiring federal agencies, under its direction, that have land management responsibilities to consider potential climate change impacts as part of long range planning endeavors.

The increase of carbon dioxide (CO_2) within the earth's atmosphere has been linked to the gradual rise in surface temperature commonly referred to as global warming. In relation to comprehensive conservation planning for national wildlife refuges, carbon sequestration constitutes the primary climate-related impact that refuges can affect in a small way. The U.S. Department of Energy's *"Carbon Sequestration Research and Development"* defines carbon sequestration as "...the capture and secure storage of carbon that would otherwise be emitted to or remain in the atmosphere."

Vegetated land is a tremendous factor in carbon sequestration. Terrestrial biomes of all sorts – grasslands, forests, wetlands, tundra, and desert – are effective both in preventing carbon emission and acting as a biological "scrubber" of atmospheric

CO_2. The Department of Energy report's conclusions noted that ecosystem protection is important to carbon sequestration and may reduce or prevent loss of carbon currently stored in the terrestrial biosphere.

Conserving natural habitat for wildlife is the heart of any long-range plan for national wildlife refuges. The actions proposed in this CCP would conserve or restore land and habitat, and would thus retain existing carbon sequestration on the Refuge. This in turn contributes positively to efforts to mitigate human-induced global climate change.

One Service activity in particular – prescribed burning – releases CO_2 directly to the atmosphere from the biomass consumed during combustion. However, there is actually no net loss of carbon, since new vegetation quickly germinates and sprouts to replace the burned-up biomass and sequesters or assimilates an approximately equal amount of carbon as was lost to the air (Boutton et al. 2006). Overall, there should be little or no net change in the amount of carbon sequestered at Rice Lake NWR from any of the proposed management alternatives.

Several impacts of climate change have been identified that may need to be considered and addressed in the future:

- Habitat available for cold water fish such as trout and salmon in lakes and streams could be reduced.

- Forests may change, with some species shifting their range northward or dying out, and other trees moving in to take their place.

- Ducks and other waterfowl could lose breeding habitat due to stronger and more frequent droughts.

- Changes in the timing of migration and nesting could put some birds out of sync with the life cycles of their prey species.

- Animal and insect species historically found farther south may colonize new areas to the north as winter climatic conditions moderate

Managers and resource specialists on the Refuge need to be aware of the possibility of change due to global warming. When feasible, documenting long-term vegetation, species, and hydrologic changes should become a part of research and monitoring programs on the Refuge. Adjustments in refuge management direction may be necessary over the course of time to adapt to a changing climate.

The following paragraphs are excerpts from the 2000 report, *Climate Change Impacts on the United States: The Potential Consequences of Climate Variability and Change*, produced by the National Assessment Synthesis Team, an advisory committee chartered under the Federal Advisory Committee Act to help the US Global Change Research Program fulfill its mandate under the Global Change Research Act of 1990. These excerpts are from the section of the report focused upon the eight-state Midwest region.

Observed Climate Trends

Over the 20th century, the northern portion of the Midwest, including the upper Great Lakes, has warmed by almost 4 degree F (2 degrees C), while the southern portion, along the Ohio River valley, has cooled by about 1 degree F (0.5 degrees C). Annual precipitation has increased, with many of the changes quite substantial, including as much as 10 to 20 percent increases over the 20th century. Much of the precipitation has resulted from an increased rise in the number of days with heavy and very heavy precipitation events. There have been moderate to very large increases in the number of days with excessive moisture in the eastern portion of the basin.

Scenarios of Future Climate

During the 21st century, models project that temperatures will increase throughout the Midwest, and at a greater rate than has been observed in the 20th century. Even over the northern portion of the region, where warming has been the largest, an accelerated warming trend is projected for the 21st century, with temperatures increasing by 5 to 10°F (3 to 6°C). The average minimum temperature is likely to increase as much as 1 to 2°F (0.5 to 1°C) more than the maximum temperature. Precipitation is likely to continue its upward trend, at a slightly accelerated rate; 10 to 30% increases are projected across much of the region. Despite the increases in precipitation, increases in temperature and other meteorological factors are likely to lead to a substantial increase in evaporation, causing a soil moisture deficit, reduction in lake and river levels, and more drought-like conditions in much of the region. In addition, increases in the proportion of precipitation coming from heavy and extreme precipitation are very likely.

Midwest Key Issues

Reduction in Lake and River Levels

Water levels, supply, quality, and water-based transportation and recreation are all climate-sensitive issues affecting the region. Despite the projected increase in precipitation, increased evaporation due to higher summer air temperatures is likely to lead to reduced levels in the Great Lakes. Of 12 models used to assess this question, 11 suggest significant decreases in lake levels while one suggests a small increase. The total range of the 11 models' projections is less than a one-foot increase to more than a five-foot decrease. A five-foot (1.5-meter) reduction would lead to a 20 to 40% reduction in outflow to the St. Lawrence Seaway. Lower lake levels cause reduced hydropower generation downstream, with reductions of up to 15% by 2050. An increase in demand for water across the region at the same time as net flows decrease is of particular concern. There is a possibility of increased national and international tension related to increased pressure for water diversions from the Lakes as demands for water increase. For smaller lakes and rivers, reduced flows are likely to cause water quality issues to become more acute. In addition, the projected increase in very heavy precipitation events will likely lead to increased flash flooding and worsen agricultural and other non-point source pollution as more frequent heavy rains wash pollutants into rivers and lakes. Lower water levels are likely to make water-based transportation more difficult with increases in the costs of navigation of 5 to 40 percent. Some of this increase will likely be offset as reduced ice cover extends the navigation season. Shoreline damage due to high lake levels is likely to decrease 40 to 80 percent due to reduced water levels.

Adaptations: A reduction in lake and river levels would require adaptations such as re-engineering of ship docks and locks for transportation and recreation. If flows decrease while demand increases, international commissions focusing on Great Lakes water issues are likely to become even more important in the future. Improved forecasts and warnings of extreme precipitation events could help reduce some related impacts.

Agricultural Shifts

Agriculture is of vital importance to this region, the nation, and the world. It has exhibited a capacity to adapt to moderate differences in growing season climate, and it is likely that agriculture would be able to continue to adapt. With an increase in the length of the growing season, double cropping, the practice of planting a second crop after the first is harvested, is likely to become more prevalent. The CO_2 fertilization effect is likely to enhance plant growth and contribute to generally higher yields. The largest increases are projected to occur in the northern areas of the region, where crop yields are currently temperature limited. However, yields are not likely to increase in all parts of the region. For example, in the southern portions of Indiana and Illinois, corn yields are likely to decline, with 10-20% decreases projected in some locations. Consumers are likely to pay lower prices due to generally increased yields, while most producers are likely to suffer reduced profits due to declining prices. Increased use of pesticides and herbicides are very likely to be required and to present new challenges.

Adaptations: Plant breeding programs can use skilled climate predictions to aid in breeding new varieties for the new growing conditions. Farmers can then choose varieties that are better attuned to the expected climate. It is likely that plant breeders will need to use all the tools of plant breeding, including genetic engineering, in adapting to climate change. Changing planting and harvest dates and planting densities, and using integrated pest management, conservation tillage, and new farm technologies are additional options. There is also the potential for shifting or expanding the area where certain crops are grown if climate conditions become more favorable. Weather conditions during the growing season are the primary factor in year-to-year differences in corn and soybean yields. Droughts and floods result in large yield reductions; severe droughts, like the drought of 1988, cause yield reductions of over 30%. Reliable seasonal forecasts are likely to help farmers adjust their practices from year to year to respond to such events.

Changes in Semi-natural and Natural Ecosystems

The upper Midwest has a unique combination of soil and climate that allows for abundant coniferous tree growth. Higher temperatures and increased evaporation will likely reduce boreal forest acreage, and make current forestlands more susceptible to pests and diseases. It is likely that the southern transition zone of the boreal forest will be susceptible to expansion of temperate forests, which in turn will have to compete with other land use pressures. However, warmer weather (coupled with beneficial effects of increased CO2),are likely to lead to an increase in tree growth rates on marginal forest-

lands that are currently temperature-limited. Most climate models indicate that higher air temperatures will cause greater evaporation and hence reduced soil moisture, a situation conducive to forest fires. As the 21st century progresses, there will be an increased likelihood of greater environmental stress on both deciduous and coniferous trees, making them susceptible to disease and pest infestation, likely resulting in increased tree mortality.

As water temperatures in lakes increase, major changes in freshwater ecosystems will very likely occur, such as a shift from cold water fish species, such as trout, to warmer water species, such as bass and catfish. Warmer water is also likely to create an environment more susceptible to invasions by non-native species. Runoff of excess nutrients (such as nitrogen and phosphorus from fertilizer) into lakes and rivers is likely to increase due to the increase in heavy precipitation events. This, coupled with warmer lake temperatures, is likely to stimulate the growth of algae, depleting the water of oxygen to the detriment of other living things. Declining lake levels are likely to cause large impacts to the current distribution of wetlands. There is some chance that some wetlands could gradually migrate, but in areas where their migration is limited by the topography, they would disappear. Changes in bird populations and other native wildlife have already been linked to increasing temperatures and more changes are likely in the future. Wildlife populations are particularly susceptible to climate extremes due to the effects of drought on their food sources.

Administrative Facilities

The major buildings on Rice Lake NWR include the Refuge headquarters/visitor contact station, two residences, a maintenance shop, and five buildings for vehicle and equipment storage (Figure 10). There are no facilities associated with the Sandstone Unit or Mille Lacs NWR.

Archeological and Cultural Values

A limited description of cultural values can be found in Historical Context, page 15. The most recent cultural resources overview of the Refuge is "A Cultural Resources Reconnaissance of Rice Lake National Wildlife Refuge, Aitkin County, Minnesota," by Oothoudt and Watson, 1978. While the Service recognizes the need for a current cultural

Figure 10: Facilities, Rice Lake NWR

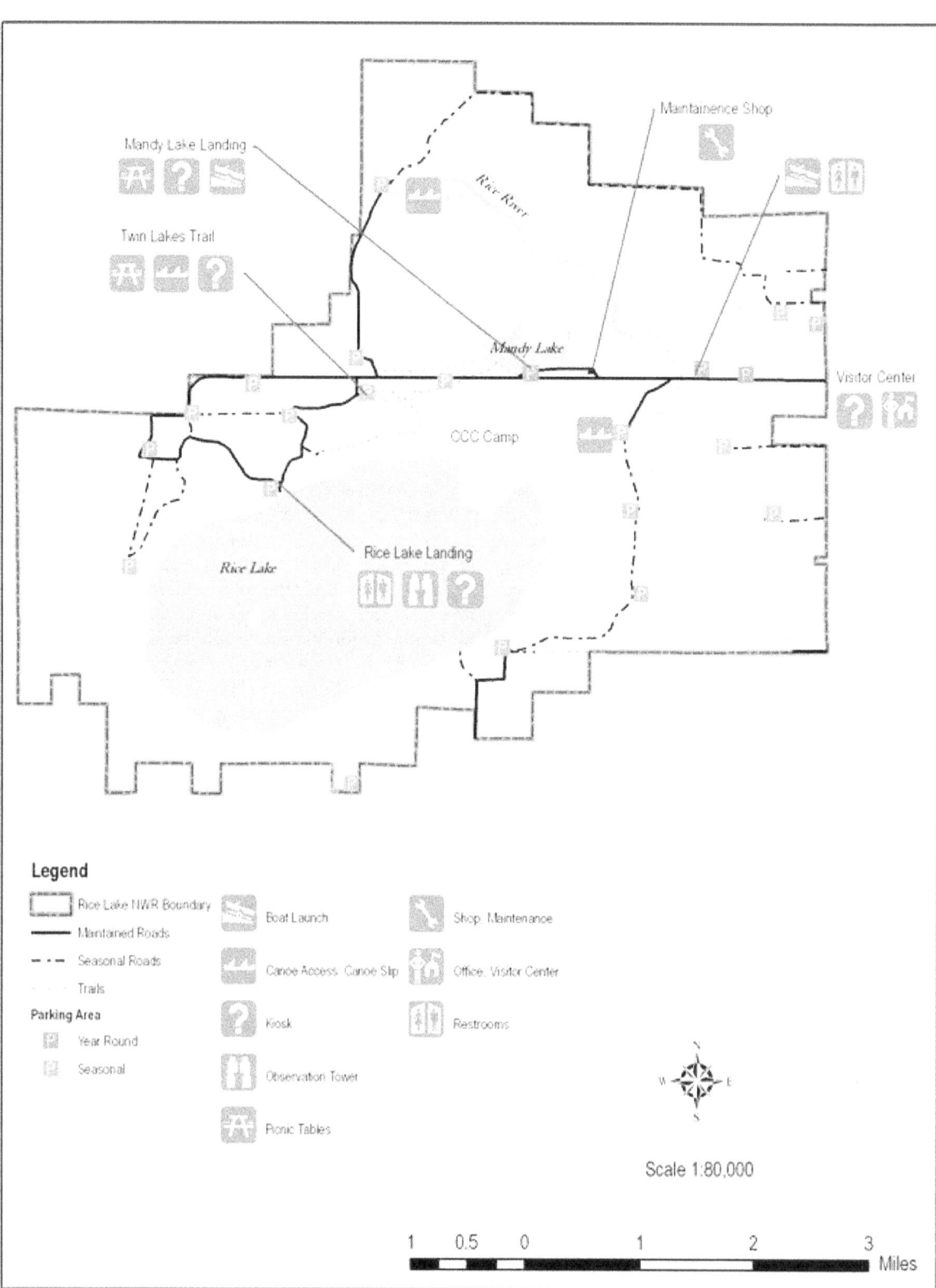

resources overview and management direction study to meet the requirement in the National Wildlife Refuge System Improvement Act of 1997 that comprehensive conservation plans include "the archaeological and cultural values of the planning unit," no such study has been completed for the entire Refuge. In partial fulfillment, the Service contracted for and obtained the "Cultural Resources Management Plan for Indian Point at Rice Lake National Wildlife Refuge" by Ollendorf, 2002.

Limited archeological investigations centered on Indian Point villages and extensive related mound groups have identified evidence of the Middle Woodland Malmo (200 B.C-A.D. 200), Saint Croix (A.D. 300-800), and Arvilla (A.D. 600-900); Late Woodland Sandy Lake (A.D. 1000-1750); and Chippewa (late 19th century-1939). Western (e.g. Euro-American) culture is also represented on the Refuge. Documents refer to sites associated with lumbering, farmsteads and fields, a Civilian Conservation Corps camp (as well as facilities on the Refuge constructed by the CCC), hunters' graves, cabins, and railroad in addition to Refuge facilities. The Refuge contains the historic Chippewa Cemetery, which continues to be used by the East Lake Band. The Refuge also has museum property and Indian interview descriptions of traditional cultural properties.

Cultural resources are important parts of the Nation's heritage. The Service is committed to protecting valuable evidence of human interactions with each other and the landscape. Protection is accomplished in conjunction with the Service's mandate to protect fish, wildlife, and plant resources.

Visitor Services

About 35,000 total visits were made to Rice Lake NWR and the Sandstone Unit in 2006. Visitation on the Refuge has been slowly increasing over the past several years. Visitors participate in wildlife observation, photography, interpretation, hunting, fishing, and environmental education. Most Refuge visitors are engaged in wildlife observation and benefit from interpretive displays located at the Visitor Contact Station and kiosks. It is estimated that fewer than 1,000 hunting visits and nearly 10,000 fishing visits occur per year. About 200 students each year experience programs on and off the Refuge. Through outreach efforts that include group presentations and exhibits, the Refuge reaches more than 5,000 people each year.

Little is known about the characteristics of Refuge visitors. The residential status of visitors was compiled using a "sign-in" book at the headquarters building for the years 2000-2004. The assumption is that repeat visitors and visitors from nearby are less likely to register in our book. However, registrants likely reflect the general origin of visitors apart from the local community. Of the visitors who signed the book, about 40 percent were from within 50 miles of the Refuge, 20 percent were from within 50-100 miles, 34 percent were from within 100-150 miles (this distance includes much of the Twin Cities metropolitan area), and 6 percent were from over 150 miles from the Refuge. Based on staff conversations with them, it is clear that visitors from more distant places are often serious bird watchers who have sought out the Refuge.

The Minnesota Department of Transportation estimated that the average daily traffic volume past the Refuge office on State Highway 65 in 2004 was 3,100 vehicles per day.

Mille Lacs NWR is closed to the public to protect the birds that use the islands from disturbance.

Current Management

Habitat Management

Current management is based on the 1997 Landscape Plan. This plan marked a change in Refuge management from the early wildlife management practice of encouraging small patchwork blocks of habitat favoring "edge" species to managing larger landscape blocks, reducing habitat fragmentation and favoring species of concern that use large blocks of unbroken habitat. The 1997 Landscape Plan also emphasized management of landscapes across Refuge boundaries by way of cooperative management agreements with other agencies and through the Private Lands program.

Wetland Management

The two major Refuge water impoundments, Rice Lake and the Rice River Pool, are managed to provide favorable food and habitat conditions for waterfowl and other wetland wildlife. Rice Lake, a large, shallow natural lake, is managed primarily for the production of wild rice. Wild rice production requires stable water levels throughout the growing season (early May to late September). Sufficient water depth is also required in Rice Lake to allow access for American Indians to harvest wild rice. The Rice River Pool is part of the Rice River and is

David Aubid ricing on Rice Lake NWR.

regulated to provide favorable conditions for growth and availability of moist soil plants, nesting waterfowl, and fall migration habitat within the pool.

Refuge (Rice Lake and Sandstone) wetland restoration projects have been completed in locations where farming once occurred and affected or eliminated naturally-occurring wetlands. During the 1950s, small water control structures called screw gates were placed on ditches in the Refuge to control water in man-made goose ponds. These gates have since been left open and the ponds have been allowed to fluctuate seasonally. Beavers have also produced some high-quality wetlands throughout the Refuge that provide nesting and migration habitat for waterbirds.

Bog Management

The Refuge has approximately 3,000 acres of bog adjacent to the Kimberly Marsh Wildlife Management Area that contains an additional 5,000 acres of bog habitat. The Refuge and the Minnesota DNR have conducted joint prescribed burn operations on this expansive bog to maximize restoration efforts in setting back the encroaching brush like willow and dogwood. These bogs, when burned periodically,

have resulted in lower brush densities that provide a more suitable habitat for Sharptail Grouse as well as for waterbird species like Yellow Rail and American Bittern for both migration and nesting purposes, and also neo-tropical migrants like the LeConte's Sparrow.

Forest Management

A vegetation inventory has been completed for Rice Lake NWR that includes a strong forest inventory component. The inventory has been started for the Sandstone Unit. Adjoining state and county lands in Aitkin County have also been inventoried and provide a good overview of the forest on a landscape level. The inventory includes eight forest types. The largest types located on Rice Lake NWR are northern hardwood forest (3,903 acres), mixed hardwood swamp (1,247 acres), and lowland hardwood forest (1,008 acres). The last permit issued to remove trees was in 1982, when approximately 6,500 board feet were cut to open up the forest canopy and to improve conditions for deer and Ruffed Grouse. Large sections of forest are managed for "old growth" and have been allowed to mature undisturbed. Logging road remnants have been sheared and mowed to facilitate access. This practice also encourages young aspen growth for Woodcock and early-successional species like Golden-winged Warblers.

Fish and Wildlife Monitoring

The monitoring surveys that are conducted on Rice Lake NWR and Mille Lacs NWR are provided in Appendix E. Birds, mammals, amphibians, fish and habitat are surveyed and monitored on regular schedules. The surveys are conducted by Refuge staff, volunteers, or in partnership with the Minnesota DNR. The purpose of monitoring is, in general, to estimate the presence/absence and numbers of fish and wildlife present and to aid in making management decisions. Analysis of the data is limited to tabulation with little statistical analysis.

Visitor Services

Mille Lacs NWR is closed to public use. Rice Lake NWR and the Sandstone Unit provide opportunities for wildlife-dependent recreation.

Law Enforcement

Protecting the visiting public, visitor use areas, cultural areas, administrative areas, residential areas, wildlife habitat, and the wildlife resources from criminal or negligent actions, as well as from acts of nature, requires that certain safeguards be in place. The Refuge maintains an automatic gate at the main entrance that closes at dusk and reopens at dawn. The gate, coupled with periodic law enforcement patrols, nearly eliminates after-hours unauthorized entries and the late night illegal activities. Law enforcement is provided by Conservation Officers from the Minnesota DNR, and Refuge law enforcement officers from other stations are also brought in to assist as needed.

Hunting

Approximately 10,000 acres of Rice Lake NWR are open to public hunting of small game and deer by archery. The areas of the Refuge near the wildlife drive and hiking trails (approximately 3,500 acres) are closed to hunting. However, during a special 9-day Refuge firearm season for deer, all of the Refuge, with the exception of a small area around the Headquarters building and the maintenance area, are open to hunting. Approximately 1,340 acres of the Sandstone Unit are open to public hunting. Approximately 705 acres on the north side of the Unit are closed to hunting and firearms due to the proximity to the federal penitentiary.

Fishing

Fishing is permitted in Twin Lakes, Mandy Lake and the Rice River during regular State seasons. Rice Lake is closed to fishing. Visitors may use motorless boats or boats with electric motors on all fishing areas. Ice fishing is permitted on Mandy Lake. However, the use of gas-powered ice augers is not allowed. Ice fishing shelters must be removed from the ice at the end of each day. Fish that are commonly caught include northern pike, yellow perch, bullhead, bigmouth buffalo, and bluegill.

Interpretation, Wildlife Observation, and Photography

The observation tower at Rice Lake provides a vista of the 18,200-acre Refuge (not including the 2,045-acre Sandstone Unit), including the 3,600-acre lake. A self-guided 9.5-mile auto tour is open to the public from dawn to dusk. Brochures are located at the Refuge Headquarters and at kiosks along the tour route. Visitors also experience the Refuge by way of hiking and cross-country skiing trails, canoeing/kayaking, snowshoeing, and biking. All trails pass through a mixture of upland and lowland hardwood forest, small grasslands and marsh. The

Environmental education at Rice Lake NWR, U.S. Fish & Wildlife Service

slope for most trails ranges from level to gently sloping.

Environmental Education

The Refuge hosts classes of elementary and high school students from local schools when teachers request visits, as well as hosting visits by home-school programs. There is no formal curriculum for Refuge programs. Programs are presented in nearby schools and the Refuge participates in educational programs like the Envirothon and Big Sandy Water Institute.

Harvesting Wild Rice

American Indians harvest a portion of the wild rice crop from the Refuge each year under a Cooperative Agreement signed in 1935.

Predator, Pest, and Invasive Species Management

Animal Species

Rice Lake NWR has a trapping program as was approved by the 2000 Furbearer Management Plan and is reviewed annually by way of the Annual Trapping Proposal. The primary purpose for a trapping program is to control the population of predators (mink, skunk, and raccoon) on ground-nesting birds and also to control nuisance muskrat and beaver, which cause damage to Refuge dikes, roads, and water control structures.

The Refuge is divided into five trapping units and special use permits are issued to trappers through a

Table 2: Trapping Statistics, Rice Lake NWR

Species	10-Year Average 1996/97 Season Through 2005/06
Beaver	33
Muskrat	44
Mink	1
Raccoon	5
Skunk	0

lottery system. Low fur prices in recent years have diminished interest in trapping on the Refuge and as a result some units are not trapped each year. The average number of trappers per season for the past 10 years is 2.7. The Refuge has adopted all State trapping regulations except where Refuge regulations are more restrictive. Trapping statistics for the past 10 years are shown in Table 2.

Plant Species

Herbicides are used to control unwanted plants in public parking areas. Mowing is used to maintain trails, secondary use roads, seasonal parking lots and road sides. The Mille Lacs Electric Company uses mowing and herbicides to maintain its right-of-way along the east edge of the Refuge and along the main Refuge road between the Headquarters and Maintenance areas. A long-term invasive weed mapping/monitoring program using GPS technology was initiated in 2006.

Archaeological and Cultural Values

The protection of cultural resources is important to the American public and essential to American Indian heritage. The Service is committed to protecting valuable evidence of human interactions with each other and the landscape. Protection is accomplished in conjunction with the Service's mandate to protect fish, wildlife, and plant resources.

Responsibilities for cultural resources management in the Service are shared between the refuge and regional office. The Regional Director has responsibility (1) for the National Historic Preservation Act Section 106 process when historic properties could be affected by Service activities, (2) issuing archeological permits, and (3) Indian tribal involvement. The Regional Historic Preservation Officer (RHPO) is responsible for advising the Regional Director about procedures, compliance, and implementation of the several cultural resources laws. The refuge manager's responsibilities include: early interaction with the RHPO about

activities that might affect cultural resources; protecting archeological sites and historic properties; monitoring archeological investigations by contractors and permittees; and reporting violations.

If a Refuge activity might have a cultural resources component, the refuge manager, early in the planning of activity, asks the RHPO to begin the Section 106 process. Then, either as part of general NEPA compliance and compatibility determinations or, if only cultural resources are involved, the refuge manager informs the public and local officials of the proposed activity and requests comments through presentations, meetings, and media notices. The manager informs the RHPO about any comments received and appropriate modifications and next steps are then specified.

Only qualified archeologists, or persons recommended by the Governor, are allowed to conduct archeological investigations and collecting on the Refuge. And, the Regional Director issues an Archaeological Resources Protection Act permit only when the investigations and collecting are in the public interest. Archeological investigations have been deemed compatible when carried out under the stipulations of the compatibility determination, which includes the issuance of a special use permit. Refuge personnel act to prevent unauthorized collecting by the public, contractors, and refuge personnel. If violations are detected, violators are cited and reported to the RHPO.

Mandy Lake overlook, Rice Lake NWR

Figure 11: Special Management Areas, Rice Lake NWR

Special Management Areas

Research Natural Area

The Refuge includes one Research Natural Area (RNA) (Rice Lake-Tamarack, SAF-38) that is about 100 acres in size (Figure 11). This administratively designated area is a part of a national network of reserved areas under various ownerships. The RNAs are intended to assist in the preservation of examples of all significant natural ecosystems for comparison with those influenced by man, to provide educational and research areas for scientists to study the ecology, successional trends, and other aspects of the natural environment, and to serve as gene pools and preserves for rare and endangered species of plants and animals. In RNAs, natural processes are allowed to predominate without human

intervention. Under certain circumstances, deliberate manipulation may be used to maintain the unique features for which the RNA was established. Activities such as wildlife-dependent recreation are permissible, but not mandated, in RNAs.

Wilderness Area

In 1973, as part of a review of all lands within the National Wildlife Refuge System, the Bureau of Sport Fisheries and Wildlife studied the potential for designation of lands within Rice Lake NWR and Mille Lacs NWR as Wilderness (USDI, Bureau of Sport Fisheries & Wildlife, 1973). As a result of the study, a 1,400-acre unit and the 6.27-acre island in Rice Lake within Rice Lake NWR (Figure 11) and the two islands of Mille Lacs NWR were recommended for further consideration by the Secretary of Interior for Wilderness designation. The study

Figure 12: Conservation Easement Areas, Rice Lake NWR

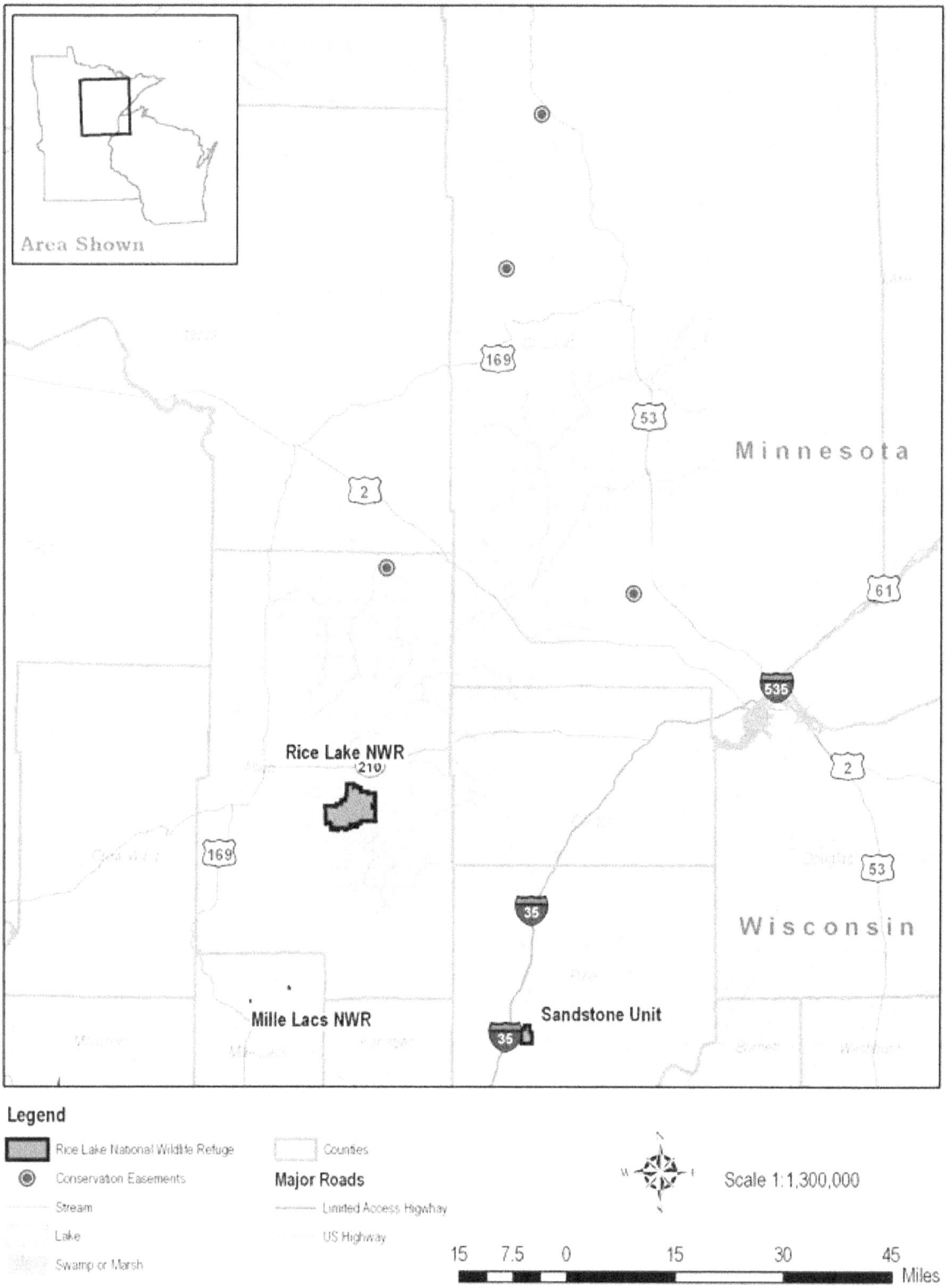

Forest in winter, Rice Lake NWR

excluded most of the Refuge from consideration because facilities or intensive management for wildlife purposes were incompatible with Wilderness designation. The Mille Lacs NWR islands have been removed from further consideration due to management actions taken for the benefit of nesting Common Terns, which altered the wilderness character of the islands. The Rice Lake NWR areas recommended for further consideration did not have roads or active manipulation of the habitat and have been managed as de facto wilderness since the study. Since the study 34 years ago, no action has been taken by the Service or Department on the findings of the Wilderness Study.

Conservation Easements

When the Farm Services Agency (FSA), formerly the Farmers Home Administration (FmHA), acquires property through default of loans, it is required to protect wetland and floodplain resources on the property prior to resale to the public. The Service assists the FSA in identifying important wetland and floodplain resources on the property. Once those resources have been identified, FSA protects the areas through a perpetual conservation easement and transfers management responsibility to the Service. The authority and direction comes from the Consolidated Farm and Rural Development Act (7 U.S.C. 1981 and 1985, as amended); Executive Order 11990 providing for the protection of wetlands; and Executive Order 11988 providing for the management of floodplain resources. The Service administers the easements as part of the National Wildlife Refuge System.

The Refuge manages four conservation easement areas totaling 362 acres located within a six-county area in northeastern Minnesota (see Figure 12). Inadequate staffing levels have impeded proper

management of the widely dispersed easements. Some of the easements have not been surveyed or marked on the ground. The easements should be inspected regularly, but some have not been inspected in over 10 years. Without appropriate monitoring the easements and their resources can not be protected from the myriad forms of encroachment.

Private Lands

Refuge biologists participate in conservation activities on private lands within the six-county area. Activities include classifying wetlands and providing technical advice on habitat restoration and management. The biologists serve as agents in promoting the programs of others with the common goal of restoring and protecting additional wildlife habitats on private lands.

Current Staff and Budget

Staff

The Refuge's staffing as of June 2006 is illustrated in Figure 13.

Budget

A 5-year history of the operating and maintenance budget for the Refuge is displayed in Table 3. The FY 2001 funding included the study of relationships between multi-scale habitat features and forest bird productivity at Rice Lake NWR. The FY 2005 funding included $90,108 for the purchase of a new dump truck.

Volunteers

Volunteers contribute valuable time and talent to all aspects of Refuge operations. They help with maintenance, construction, wildlife and resource monitoring, interpretation, and public contact. Over the 5 years from 2000 to 2004, the number of hours volunteers contributed to the Refuge ranged from 587 to 2,060 per year. Some volunteers live in nearby communities with one-way travel times of one hour; others travel from as far away as New Mexico and Indiana and stay in their personally owned RVs.

Figure 13: Staffing Chart, Rice Lake NWR

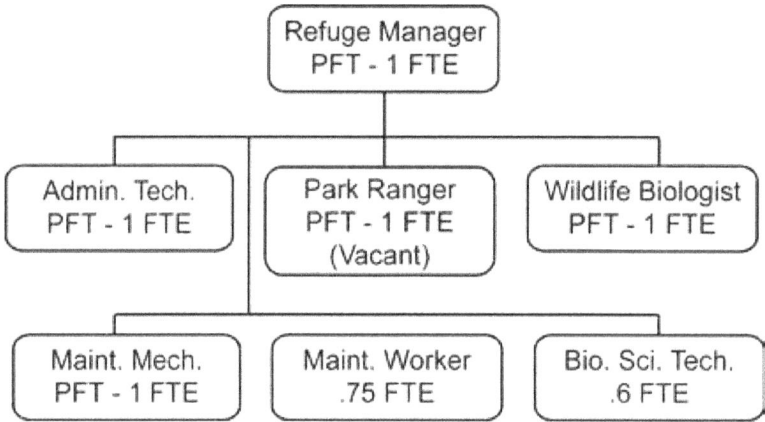

Table 3: 5-Year Annual Operating and Maintenance Funding

Funding	FY 2001	FY 2002	FY 2003	FY 2004	FY 2005
Private Lands	$7,000	$10,021	$0	$0	$0
Non-game and Engineering	$10,000	$1,500	$0	$400	$3,000
Salaries and Operation	$409,184	$370,649	$454,483	$407,123	$509,500
Maintenance	$71,000	$214,000	$180,916	$82,401	$132,700
Fire	$35,918	$30,406	$55,866	$66,789	$45,200

Partnerships

The Refuge has many partnerships that foster community relations and enhance Refuge habitats and wildlife populations. Recent partners include:

- Minnesota Department of Natural Resources (Divisions of Ecological Services, Wildlife, Parks, Fisheries, Forestry, Enforcement, and the Aitkin Area Ecosystem Team)
- U.S. Department of Agriculture (NRCS, FSA)
- Aitkin County Soil and Water Conservation District
- Big Sandy Area Watershed Task Force
- Aitkin County Forest Advisory Committee
- Long Lake Conservation Center
- Aitkin County Water Planning Task Force
- Aitkin County Land Department
- Aitkin County Sheriff
- Palisade Volunteer Fire Department
- Mille Lacs Band of Ojibwe (DNR, Police)
- University of Minnesota
- Central Lakes College

- McGregor Area Planning Committee
- Rivers and Lakes Fair Planning Committee
- McGregor Chamber of Commerce
- Wetland Conservation Act Advisory Committee
- Big Sandy Water Institute
- Minnesota Audubon
- Bee Nay She Birding Council
- Minnesota Historical Society, for curation and storage of four archeological collections totaling 1,257 artifacts from the Refuge.

A special partnership exists with the non-profit group, Friends of Rice Lake Refuge, which formed in October 2002. The Friends have approximately 100 members. The Friends support and enhance the public's role in fish and wildlife habitat protection. Their goal is to promote public use along with educating visitors on the natural and cultural resources of the area. The group has sponsored events and built facilities on the Refuge and represented the Refuge at community and county gatherings. The Friends operate the sales area in the visitor contact station.

Chapter 4: Refuge Management

Introduction

Goals and Objectives

The goals that follow are general statements of what the Refuge wants to accomplish. The objectives under each goal are specific statements of what will be accomplished to help achieve the goal. Strategies listed under each objective specify the activities that will be pursued to realize an objective. The strategies may be refined or amended as specific tasks are completed or new research and information come to light.

Rice Lake National Wildlife Refuge

Goal 1:

The Refuge will contain a diversity of habitats typical of historical north-central Minnesota. (See Figure 14 on page 42)

(The Sandstone Unit habitat community objectives are listed separately, see Objective 1.10.)

Forest Community

Objective 1.1: Forest Size

Restore and maintain between 8,000 and 10,500 acres of diverse forest types.

Rationale: The Refuge has about 7,100 acres of forest habitat. Studies have shown that forest fragmentation reduces nesting success of migratory birds because of increased nest predation and parasitism. By managing the Refuge's forest in coordination with neighbors and partners, large blocks can be created. The Refuge forest

Rice Lake on Rice Lake NWR

will be a mosaic of hardwoods with scattered pines and patches of aspen. The forest structure will not be constant throughout. Variability will be introduced by natural disturbance and management activities. The mixed forest with diverse plant forms, vertical structures, and ages will provide habitat for a wide variety of wildlife. The priority bird species that are expected to benefit from mixed-age stands are neotropical species like Golden-winged Warblers and game species like American Woodcock. The bird species that are expected to benefit from reduced fragmentation are forest-interior birds such as Wood Thrush, Red-eyed Vireo, Scarlet Tanager, Ovenbird, Pileated Woodpecker, and Broad-winged Hawk.

Strategies:

1. Convert 50 percent of small forest openings within the forested communities by 2020 through planting or succession.

2. Maintain forest continuity with Aitkin County lands that are adjacent to the south Refuge boundary.

Figure 14: Future Desired Landcover, Rice Lake NWR

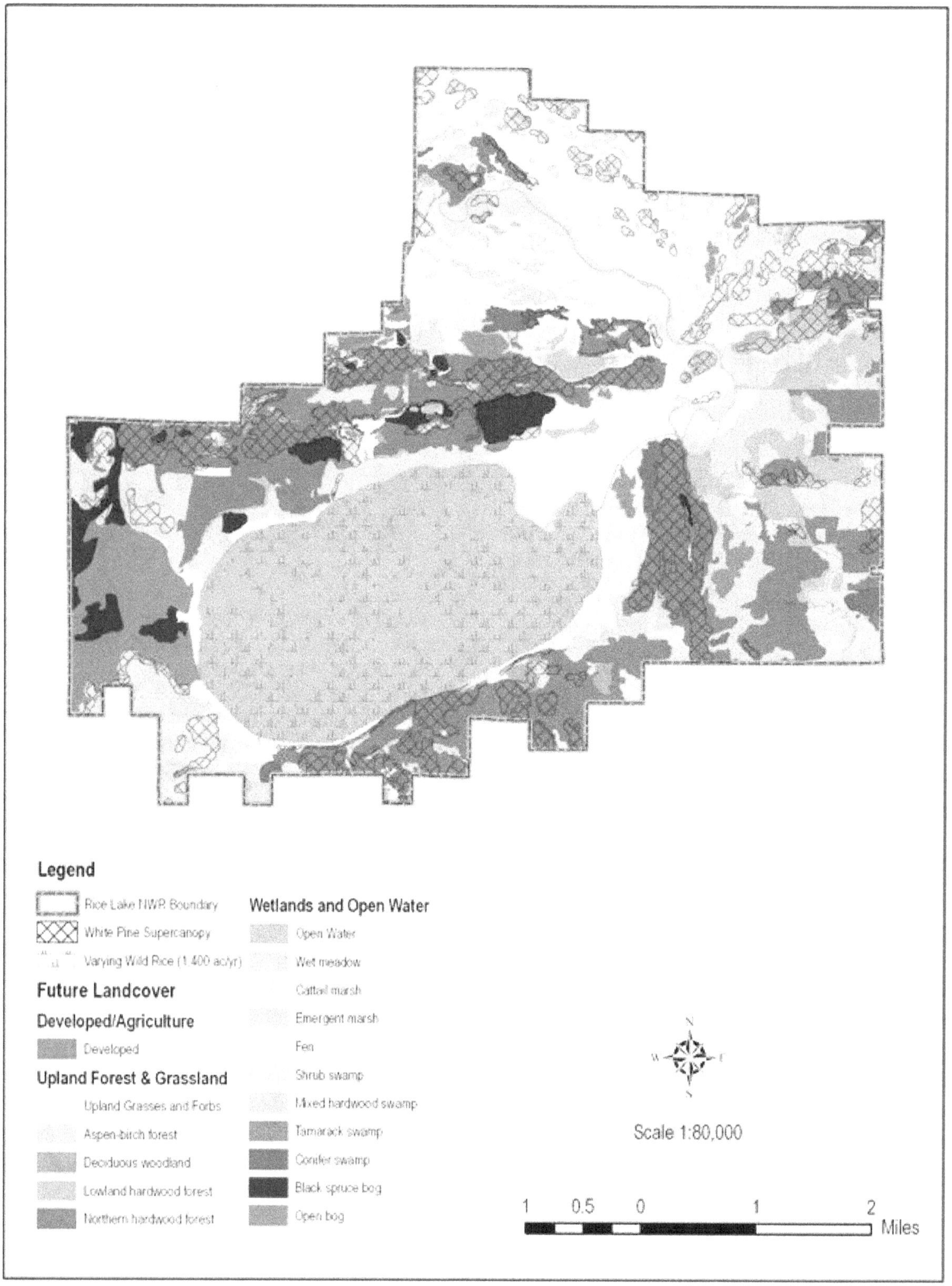

Legend

☐ Rice Lake NWR Boundary

▨ White Pine Supercanopy

░ Varying Wild Rice (1,400 ac/yr)

Future Landcover

Developed/Agriculture

■ Developed

Upland Forest & Grassland

Upland Grasses and Forbs

Aspen-birch forest

Deciduous woodland

Lowland hardwood forest

Northern hardwood forest

Wetlands and Open Water

Open Water

Wet meadow

Cattail marsh

Emergent marsh

Fen

Shrub swamp

Mixed hardwood swamp

Tamarack swamp

Conifer swamp

Black spruce bog

Open bog

Scale 1:80,000

1   0.5   0   1   2 Miles

3. Develop a forest plan as part of more detailed habitat management planning by 2008.

Objective 1.2: Conifer Component

By the year 2106, have a 10 white pine/acre component on all suitable sites of a super-canopy size. To achieve this long-term objective, while allowing for attrition, increase the amount of white pine on suitable sites of any age class to ~14 white pine/acre, through natural regeneration and planting by 2020.

Rationale: White pine and, to a lesser degree, red pine were very abundant in the pre-settlement mixed forests of the region. Logging in the late 1800s eliminated all except the smallest of pine trees, making way for the mixed hardwood forests seen today. In the subsections that include the Refuge, white pine has declined 5-10 fold since the late 1800s. To mimic historic conditions it is desirable to reestablish white pine as a component of Refuge mixed forests and to reestablish the forest super-canopy layer on sites with the right environmental conditions. A super-canopy consists of white pines that are taller than 75 feet, which tend to be trees with a DBH (Diameter of Breast Height) of 16 inches or more. A variety of strategies will need to be used to establish white pines because the nature of the suitable sites varies. The priority bird species that are expected to benefit from the conifers as part of the mixed forest are large raptors such as Bald Eagles and mammals such as black bears.

Strategies:

1. Determine and map sites suitable for conifer restoration.

2. Establish conifers on suitable sites through natural regeneration or planting with site preparation and management that may include mixed conifer planting, prescribed fire, selective harvesting, and brush control.

3. By 2010, plant 20 percent of suitable areas without a white pine component at a rate of 25 white pine seedlings/acre. An expected mortality rate of 25 percent over 40 years reduces the amount to ~14 white pine/acre by 2050.

4. By 2020, plant all remaining suitable areas without a white pine component at a rate of 25 white pine seedlings/acre. An expected mortality rate of 25 percent over 40 years reduces the amount to ~14 white pine/acre by 2060.

5. Manage both planted and natural regeneration sites to protect seedlings from whitetail deer browsing and disease through bud capping, repellants, and pruning.

Objective 1.3: Northern Hardwoods

Manage northern hardwood habitat as an uneven age system for a diversity of structure, tending toward early successional stages in some areas currently dominated by aspen, and tending toward later successional ecosystems in areas dominated by maple/basswood.

Rationale: Management should strive to retain critical ecosystem/cover/habitat types (Holling and Meffe 1996) as well as focus on maintaining overall biodiversity and maintain or restore ecosystem/habitat diversity and function (Lambeck 1997). At the landscape scale, management should maintain the diversity of cover types and seral stages, and increase mean patch size (Crozier and Niemi 2003). Aspen was part of the historic forest and emerged in patches where trees had been lost though fire or windthrow. Species expected to benefit from the early successional stages of aspen (DeGraaf and Yamaski, 2003) include:

- Golden-winged Warbler
- Northern Flicker
- Olive-sided Flycatcher
- Winter Wren
- Eastern bluebird
- Chestnut-sided Warbler
- Black-and-white Warbler
- Mourning Warbler
- Canada Warbler
- White-throated Sparrow
- Rose-breasted Grosbeak

White-tail deer fawn, Rice Lake NWR

Rice Lake, U.S. Fish & Wildlife Service

- Ruffed Grouse
- American Woodcock

Older seral stages were also a part of the historic forest. Species that benefit from older seral stages include:

- Northern Goshawk
- Bald Eagle
- Black-billed Cuckoo
- Northern Flicker
- Red-headed Woodpecker
- Wood Duck
- Wood Thrush

Strategies:

1. Determine best management tools to develop uneven-aged systems. The tools will likely include timber harvesting, maintaining aspen stands with even-age management while selectively harvesting or performing shelterwood harvest in other northern hardwood stands to create a more diverse composition of species, ages and structure.

2. Specify details of northern hardwood management in the forest portion of the habitat management plan by 2008.

3. Continue working with the Aitkin County Land Department to develop cooperative forest management objectives that provide for sustained and diverse wildlife benefits.

Objective 1.4: Coniferous Bog

Maintain 1,000 acres of coniferous bog where it currently occurs.

Rationale: Pristine lowland forest is a declining habitat in northern Minnesota. The Refuge contains black spruce, white cedar and tamarack in their natural condition associated with true bogs containing important plant species like orchids, sedges, and those that are carnivorous. These bog areas are important habitat to migrating and breeding neo-tropical migrants like the Connecticut Warbler and Yellow-bellied Flycatcher.

Strategies:

1. Protect stands from fire as feasible and exclude from prescribed burn units where practical.

2. Harvest trees only to control disease.

Bog Community

Objective 1.5: Open Bogs

Restore 5,000 acres of open bog (wet meadow) with a brush stem density of 6 or less stems per square meter within 15 years.

Rationale: The large expanses of open bogs on Rice Lake are typified by sedge species, a habitat type important to Sharp-tailed Grouse as well as many waterbird species, including Yellow Rail and American Bittern, and many of the neo-tropical migrants, including LeConte's Sparrow, for both migration and nesting habitat. These open "sedge bogs" would have been clear of brush and contained only islands of tamarack, spruce and cedar trees. Since settlement times, fire, the main tool in maintaining an open bog, has been suppressed, allowing for the invasion of undesirable brush species. The target of 5,000 acres is derived from the vegetation map developed for this CCP (Figure 14 on page 42).

Strategies:

1. Map sedge fen, open bog, and forested islands.

2. The frequent use of prescribed fire will be required to control brush species that have been allowed to encroach into the open bogs. The resulting frequency of fire intervals will be unnatural and potentially devastating to the forested islands. Caution will be taken to avoid the frequent burning of the forested islands when possible.

3. Continue working with the Minnesota DNR to cooperatively use prescribed fire to increase bog restoration effects on adjoining land management units with approximately 8,000 total acres.

4. Monitor effects of fire using the protocol as written in the National Park Service's Fire Monitoring Handbook.

Aquatic Community

Objective 1.6: Pickerelweed

Reduce pickerelweed occurrence by approximately 50 percent on Rice Lake to no more than 400 acres by 2015.

Rationale: Pickerelweed has significantly increased in Rice Lake over the last 40 years. This perennial, although native, is out-competing wild rice, which is a major food resource for the fall flight of migrating ducks in Minnesota. Wild rice is an annual grass that depends on disturbances like flooding to remove competing vegetation early in the spring before the rice seeds germinate. If major flooding occurs after germination of the rice seeds, plants are often uprooted and killed. Stable water levels over the last several decades at the Refuge have maintained good rice production. However, the stable water levels have also benefited pickerelweed, which is encroaching on wild rice beds. Because wild rice is important to migrating ducks and the traditional harvest by Ojibwe people, we will reduce the beds of pickerelweed in an effort to increase the size of wild rice beds.

Strategies:

1. Evaluate methods of controlling pickerelweed, including mowing as suggested by the University of Minnesota.

2. During the 10-year period immediately following approval of this plan, manipulate water levels as an experimental control method of pickerelweed. Experiments will examine the effects of both high water and low water manipulation and mimicking otherwise naturally occurring environmental conditions. Sound monitoring techniques will help develop a long-term water management plan to effectively reduce pickerelweed and maintain healthy wild rice beds. This strategy will require sacrificing wild rice production for an estimated 3 or 4 years out of 10. If no positive results are derived at the end of the

10-year period, the experiment will be terminated immediately. This strategy is linked to Objective 1.8; Strategy 3 and Objective 4.1; Strategy 3.

3. Measure size and distribution of pickerelweed beds at a minimum of 5-year intervals with scientifically credible methods.

Objective 1.7: Wild Rice

Maintain the long-term viability of wild rice on Rice Lake through 2020 with a 10-year average of 1,400 acres, 80 seeds per head, and a stem density within rice beds of at least 20 stems per square meter.

Rationale: Wild rice is a key resource to the wildlife mission and cultural heritage of the Refuge and it is central to the Refuge vision. There isn't a clear understanding of cause and effect of rice management in the lake. During the 3-year span from 2002-2004, only 2 years were considered good rice years. For the 21 years between 1983 and 2004 the acreage of the wild rice bed ranged from a low of 1,142 to a high of 1,698 with an average of 1,433. Over the 3-year period there was an average of 85 seeds per head and an average of 25 stems per square meter. The Refuge will adapt management of the rice beds as information is gathered by way of monitoring activities.

Strategies:

1. Measure the stem density and number of seeds per head at a minimum of 3-year intervals with scientifically credible methods.

2. Determine extent of rice beds with aerial photography annually.

3. Over the next 10 years, experiment with water level manipulations that mimic natural variations. Monitor results to guide future water level manipulation as a tool to increase long-term wild rice production on Rice Lake. This strategy is linked to Objective 4.1; Strategy 3.

Invasive Species

Objective 1.8: Invasive Species

Exotic invasive species will impact no more than 10 percent of the Refuge by the year 2020.

Rationale: Invasive species are considered one of the greatest threats to the National Wildlife Refuge System, and to Rice Lake NWR. The list of presently known invasive plant species includes common reed, reed canary grass, leafy spurge, and European buckthorn. European earthworms are also in Rice Lake NWR. It is probably only a matter of time before such species as purple loosestrife, spotted knapweed, Gypsy moth (100 miles distant), emerald ash borer (700 miles distant), zebra mussel (40 miles distant), common carp, Asian carp, and the New Zealand mud snail (50 miles distant) also appear. It is imperative that new invasive species populations be detected and treated quickly to reduce their impact on habitat and native wildlife populations.

Strategies:

1. Survey and map exotic invasive plant species on the Refuge that could likely cause negative impacts to the habitat. Early detection will provide for an effective and rapid response.

2. Monitor known invasive plant populations to assist in prioritization of treatment.

3. Reduce acreage of impacting invasive plant species through treatment as quickly as possible. Effective treatments may include spraying of herbicides, introduction of biological control agents, mowing, flooding, prescribed burning, cutting, hand pulling, or a combination of these treatments.

4. Find reported European buckthorn population through aerial detection by 2008.

5. Eradicate European buckthorn population through cutting, hand pulling, and herbicide application by 2010.

6. Add European earthworm detection to forest inventory protocol by 2008.

7. Map areas of earthworm populations and forested areas already showing negative impacts by 2020.

8. Monitor/assess carp issues (common carp and Asian carp) and work with Minnesota DNR Fisheries and Tribal Fisheries in developing a strategy to protect Rice Lake from the potentially devastating effects non-native carp would have on wild rice production while protecting native fisheries, using the best available science.

9. Determine effective treatment for common reed and reduce acreage by 50 percent by the year 2015.

Mushrooms, Rice Lake NWR

10. Maintain or improve the health of Refuge forests through active forest management (may include selective harvest, planting, and prescribed fire) to minimize long-term impacts caused by gypsy moth.

11. Continue annual gypsy moth detection trap monitoring and coordination with Minnesota Department of Agriculture.

12. Educate the public about invasive species and how they can help reduce the spread of invasives.

13. Hire a biological technician.

Special Management Area

Objective 1.9: Special Management Area

Withdraw consideration for Wilderness designation on 1,406 acres.

Rationale: Recommendation for consideration as Wilderness occurred in 1973. The recommendation has not been acted upon during the interceding 34 years. Refuge staff have concluded that the recommendation is no longer appropriate because the area fails to meet numerous criteria that were established to determine Wilderness suitability: it is less than 5,000 acres in size; human alterations to the habitat is readily apparent on portions of the area; it offers little opportunity for primitive recreational activities other than hunting; and it does not contain significant ecological, geological, scientific, educational, scenic, or historical features. Removing the Wilderness recommendation will allow for a complete range of management options to restore altered and/or degraded wildlife habitat.

Strategies:

1. Use this CCP as the decision document to withdraw the previous Wilderness recommendation.

2. Upon the CCP becoming final, explore available management options to the area previously managed as de facto wilderness.

Objective 1.10: Sandstone Unit

Maintain the 2005 landcover while allowing for forest succession.

Rationale: Because the Unit is 52 miles from the headquarters and maintenance shop, frequent and active management activities are not efficient. Vehicular access to the Unit is limited. Given the limited Refuge budget and higher priority needs on the main Refuge, management activities on the Sandstone Unit will continue to be limited. It is likely that prescribed burns will be the only management activity for the foreseeable future. Prescribed burning will suppress brush encroachment and maintain the open lands. The forest of the Unit is considered healthy and diverse and therefore will be allowed to succeed under natural conditions (Figure 15).

The Service will explore an exchange of the Sandstone Unit for State lands with the State of Minnesota. The purpose of the exchange will be to increase management efficiency for both entities and more closely align lands with the agencies' missions. Land exchanges are complex and require a number of years to complete. If and when the details of a possible exchange are specified, an environmental review of the proposed exchange will be completed. The environmental review process will include public notification and an opportunity for public comment.

Viewing scope, Rice Lake NWR

Strategies:

1. Incorporate prescribed burn units of the Sandstone Unit into the Refuge's burn program by 2008.

Goal 2:

Fish and migrating and resident wildlife populations on the Refuge will be naturally diverse, healthy, and self sustaining.

Objective 2.1: Regional Conservation Priority (RCP) Species

Seventy percent of all the Region 3 RCP (Appendix C) species associated with historically occurring habitats on the Refuge will occur on the Refuge by 2020. This includes 84 percent of the RCP bird species during migration or nesting.

Rationale: Region 3's RCP list includes rare and declining species, federally listed, and recreationally important species that are of high concern in the Upper Midwest. The RCP list was developed to help prioritize management within the Region. Knowing that the species are using the habitats on the Refuge will be an indicator of success in providing for these species, with the exception of nuisance species. As of 2006, the Refuge hosted 47 of 56 bird species, 1 of 1 mammal species, 0 of 2 fish species, 0 of 10 mollusk or crustacean species, and 0 of 1 insect species on the Region 3 RCP list. Numbers may change as new species are documented and as habitats are restored.

Monitoring is a key element in determining if Refuge management is achieving its goals of providing habitat for key wildlife species. Monitoring can be costly if high precision is sought. For this plan we think an initial attempt to monitor birds should have the moderate goals specified in the strategy.

Strategies:

1. Every 5 years estimate species composition and abundance of RCP waterfowl, forest and marsh birds on the Refuge with scientifically credible data of known quality. The estimation will document at least 90 percent of the species and be able to detect at least a 10 percent change in abundance over 15 years

2. Support research activities that are directed toward Region 3 RCP bird species.

3. Continue to document observed fish and wildlife species and add to existing Refuge species lists.

Figure 15: Future Desired Landcover, Sandstone Unit of Rice Lake NWR

Legend

[P] Parking Area

[ ] Sandstone Unit

Future Vegetation

Developed/Agriculture

Developed

Upland Grasses and Forbs

Upland Forest

Deciduous woodland

Lowland hardwood forest

Mixed forest

Northern hardwood forest

Wetlands and Open Water

Open Water

Wet meadow

Shrub swamp

Mixed hardwood swamp

Scale 1:30,000

0.25 0.125 0 0.25 0.5 0.75 1 Miles

Objective 2.2: Monitoring

Verify wildlife response to habitat changes and monitor populations over time with scientifically credible data.

Rationale: Following the rationale of Schroeder, King, and Cornely (1998), the Refuge's core management direction is based on habitat objectives. Schroeder et al. reason that many factors affect wildlife populations and many of these factors are outside the control of a refuge manager. However, a refuge manager can work to provide a high quality habitat, which is necessary for an abundant wildlife population. Still, at some point it is necessary to determine if wildlife is responding as envisioned.

Strategies:

1. Monitor Region 3 RCP species every 5 years through nationally recognized protocols and link results to regional and national databases.

2. Record habitat treatments in a Refuge and regional GIS database.

3. Link the wildlife and habitat data to determine differences between habitat treatment types and changes in wildlife abundance over time.

4. Increasing habitat restoration and monitoring will require the addition of a Biological Technician.

5. Hire a Biological Technician.

Goal 3:

Visitors will enjoy wildlife-dependent recreation and they, along with residents of the local community, will appreciate the value and need for fish and wildlife conservation.

Objective 3.1: Wildlife Observation and Photography

Within 5 years of approval of the plan, increase opportunities for wildlife observation and photography to correspond with a 20 percent increase (from 2005 level) in Refuge visitation.

Rationale: Little information exists about Refuge visitors. Estimates of Refuge visitation are based on two traffic counters on the Wildlife Drive. The needs and satisfaction of visitors are known only from chance conversations with visitors. In addition, local tourism and Refuge visitation is expected to increase by up to 20 percent. Scientifically sound visitor surveys would provide better

Environmental education, Rice Lake NWR

information for improving visitor opportunities. The procedures used to conduct proper visitor surveys are time consuming and costly. Therefore, basic data will be obtained within the constraints of limited Refuge resources. Additional traffic counters will be strategically placed within the Refuge to determine the types of activities visitors are enjoying. The number of people contacted at both on- and off-Refuge events will continue to be recorded.

People will be able to spend more time engaged in wildlife observation and photography if more pull-offs are available on the wildlife drive. Visitors may stay longer and enjoy their visit more if improvements are made to the public areas and wildlife drive. Longer visits may lead to a greater appreciation of the value and need for fish and wildlife conservation and the Refuge. Increased visitation will be used as an indicator that more people are learning about and appreciating the opportunities available on the Refuge. All facilities will be made accessible according to ADA standards.

Strategies:

1. Develop and implement a visitor survey if funding is available.

2. Install, monitor and maintain accurate traffic counters.

3. Add three additional pull-offs to the Wildlife Drive.

Indian pipe, Rice Lake NWR

Objective 3.2: Interpretation

Within 10 years of approval of the plan, increase opportunities for interpretation of Refuge wildlife and habitats to correspond to a 20 percent increase (from 2005 level) in Refuge visitation.

Rationale: With increased visitation comes an opportunity to interpret Refuge resources and educate a diverse group of visitors about conservation. Many people use the hiking trails, but may not be aware of the wildlife and resources they are viewing on their hikes. An interpretive trail at Twin Lakes and a kiosk at the South Trail dam will help to orient visitors and interpret the Refuge resources they will see. Visitors will spend more time learning about the Refuge and its purpose from interpretive panels if more are provided. If people stay longer on the Refuge, it may lead to a greater appreciation of the value and need for fish and wildlife conservation. Having the visitor center open on Saturdays will allow more interaction with visitors and opportunities for impromptu interpretation of Refuge resources. All facilities will be accessible according to ADA standards. (Figure 16)

1. Convert Twin Lakes trail to an interpretive trail.
2. Install a kiosk at the South Trail dam to interpret forest ecology and wildlife of the Rice River.
3. Develop and increase interpretive programs/themes through partners and a Refuge park ranger.
4. Staff the visitor center on Saturdays.
5. Hire a seasonal (7 months) park ranger/visitor services specialist.

Objective 3.3: Environmental Education

Within 2 years of hiring a park ranger/visitor services specialist, provide environmental education programming to no fewer than 600 students per year. Eighty percent of students will report an increased desire to protect fish and wildlife habitats as a result of the programs.

Rationale: Incorporating environmental education into the school curricula is an important way to influence the future well-being of the Refuge. Only through understanding and appreciation will people be moved to personal and collective action to ensure a healthy Refuge for the future. Environmental education is important in forming general conservation attitudes and responsible conduct on the Refuge.

In the past the Refuge has not offered environmental education opportunities, but responded to special requests. This objective aims to move the Refuge's environmental education program toward more action. The more active approach will depend on additional staff and resources devoted to visitor services. Because the Refuge has no history of offering environmental education and little participation data, the beginning objective has been set at 600 K-12 students in Aitkin County and the western portion of Carlton County.

Strategies:

1. Adapt existing Refuge curriculums (e.g. Rhythms of the Refuge) to Rice Lake NWR.
2. Hire a park ranger/visitor services specialist.
3. Offer a teacher workshop annually.
4. Promote the environmental education opportunities to local teachers.
5. Partner with one local school to focus efforts there.

Objective 3.4: Fishing

Within 7 years of approval of the plan, reliably determine the number of fishing visits to the Refuge and that at least 85 percent of the anglers judge that they are being provided a quality opportunity.

Rationale: Approximately 10,000 fishing visits occur on the Refuge each year. The accuracy of this number needs to be determined as well as how anglers rate their visit. The intent of this objective is to gain a reliable estimate of the number of visitors who fish and their rating of the quality of opportunities provided. This information will help determine

Figure 16: Current and Future Visitor Services Facilities, Rice Lake NWR

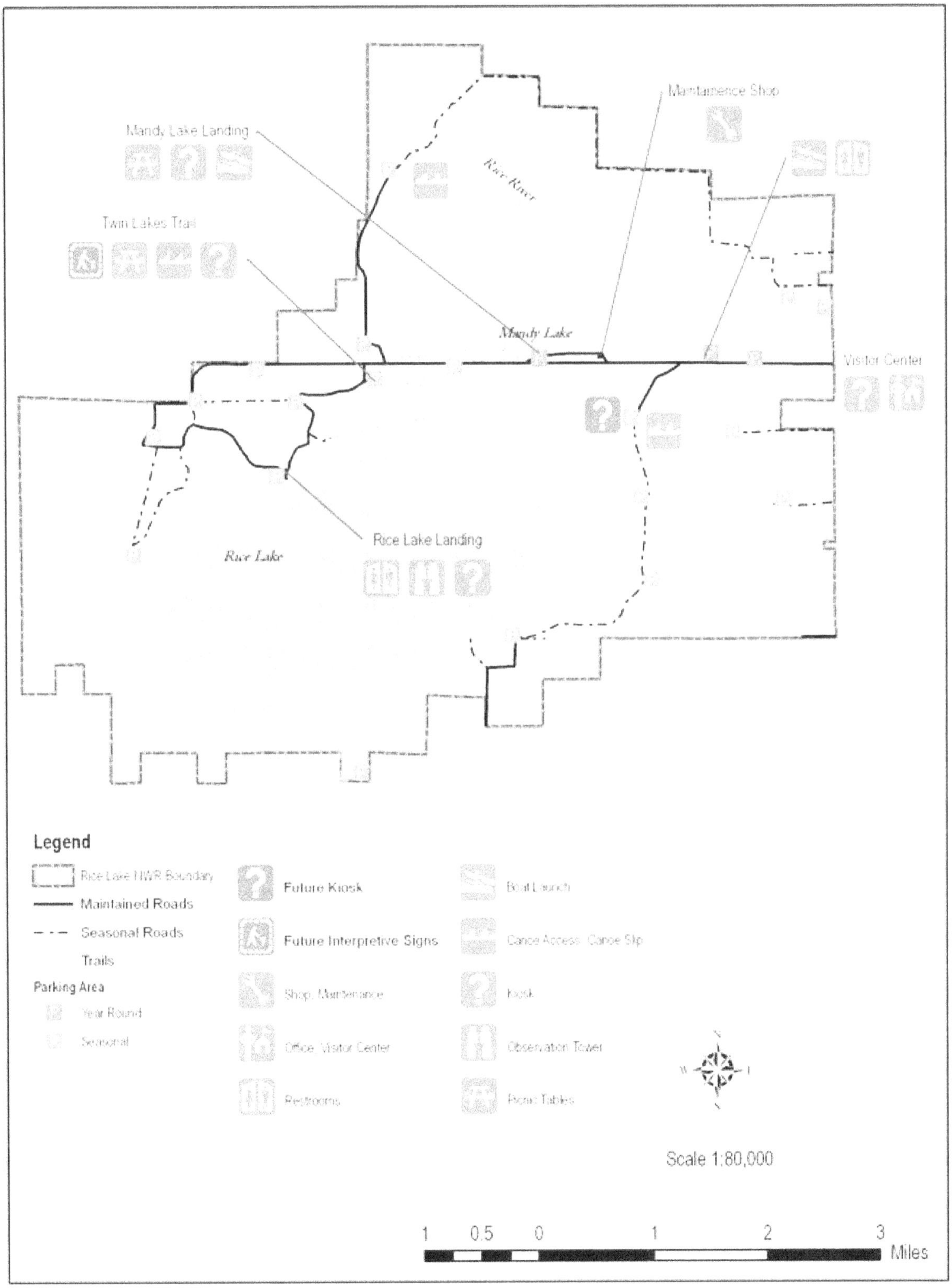

if wildlife-dependent recreational goals of the Refuge and the National Wildlife Refuge System are being met.

Strategies:

1. Develop and implement a visitor survey.

2. Maintain and improve facilities that support fishing opportunities and meet ADA standards.

3. Conduct fish census surveys at Mandy Lake and Twin Lakes to determine the viability of fish stocking efforts as a means to improve/increase fishing opportunities.

4. Conduct Fishing Week activities.

5. Provide adequate law enforcement for visitor safety and resource protection through continued cooperation with Minnesota DNR and partnerships with other refuges.

Objective 3.5: Hunting

Within 7 years of approval of the plan, reliably determine the number of hunting visits to the Refuge and that at least 85 percent of hunters judge that they are being provided a quality opportunity.

Rationale: It is estimated that the Refuge hosts fewer than 1,000 hunting visits each year. There is an opportunity to improve the hunting program by redefining the hunting areas, offering additional hunting opportunities, clarifying boundaries, and redesigning hunt brochures. By doing this, the number of hunters on the Refuge is expected to increase while maintaining quality opportunities and sufficient wildlife populations. Wildlife surveys indicate that certain populations (e.g. white-tailed deer and Ruffed Grouse) can support additional hunting pressure. This increased participation will lead to increased appreciation of national wildlife refuges.

Strategies:

1. Develop and implement a visitor survey.

2. Review hunt program opportunities and/or impacts on other programs.

3. Offer a muzzle-loader deer hunt.

4. Modify and clarify hunt boundaries for consistency, minimizing conflicts between user groups. Two hunting units will be open on the Refuge, designated as Unit A and Unit B (Figure 17). Unit A is approximately 10,503 acres and is open for small game and big

game hunting. Unit B is approximately 3,669 acres and is open to specialized hunts only (i.e. disabled access hunts, youth hunts, or special management hunts), for both big game and small game. Approximately 98 acres of land is designated as administrative areas and is closed to hunting. The hunting unit for the Sandstone Unit is depicted in Figure 18.

5. Redesign and rewrite the hunt brochure to incorporate changes to the hunt boundaries and to meet graphics standards.

6. Initiate additional special hunts for hunters with physical disabilities and a youth hunt.

7. Provide adequate law enforcement for visitor safety and resource protection through continued cooperation with the Minnesota DNR and partnerships with other Refuges.

Objective 3.6: Outreach

Within 3 years of approval of the plan increase local community support and appreciation for fish and wildlife conservation and endorse the Refuge's role in conservation.

Rationale: The Refuge considers its neighbors and visitors to be very important. The Refuge is an asset to the community and the continued support of the community is essential. It is important that the Refuge continues efforts to build and maintain open communications with neighbors to let them know the successes, challenges, and opportunities in conservation and wildlife-dependent recreation. In an ideal setting, the objective would be to achieve an appreciation of the value and need for fish and wildlife conservation among a larger percentage of the population living around the Refuge.

The success in achieving the objective would be determined through a survey of the general population. However, for an objective to be useful it must be measurable in both a conceptual and practical sense. It is not practical to propose that the Refuge will conduct a survey of the general population anytime in the next few years, because the approvals and costs are beyond the likely resources of the Refuge. As an alternative, the objective reflects the assumption that community leaders reflect and help form the attitude within the community. By evaluating the opinions of community leaders, there will be a surrogate measure of our desired outcome within the guidelines of the Office of Management and Budget.

Figure 17: Rice Lake NWR Hunt Units

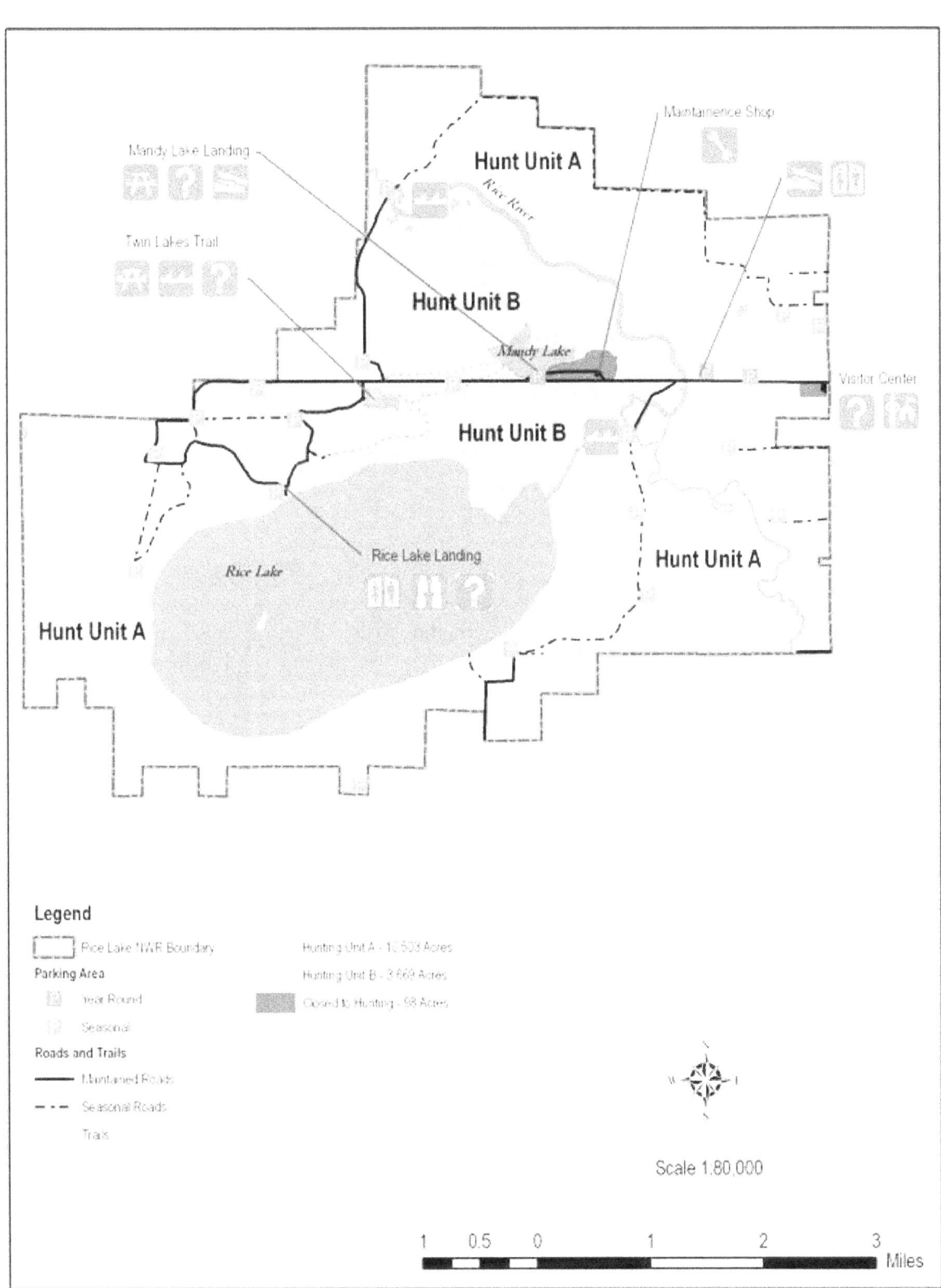

Figure 18: Sandstone Unit of Rice Lake NWR Hunt Units

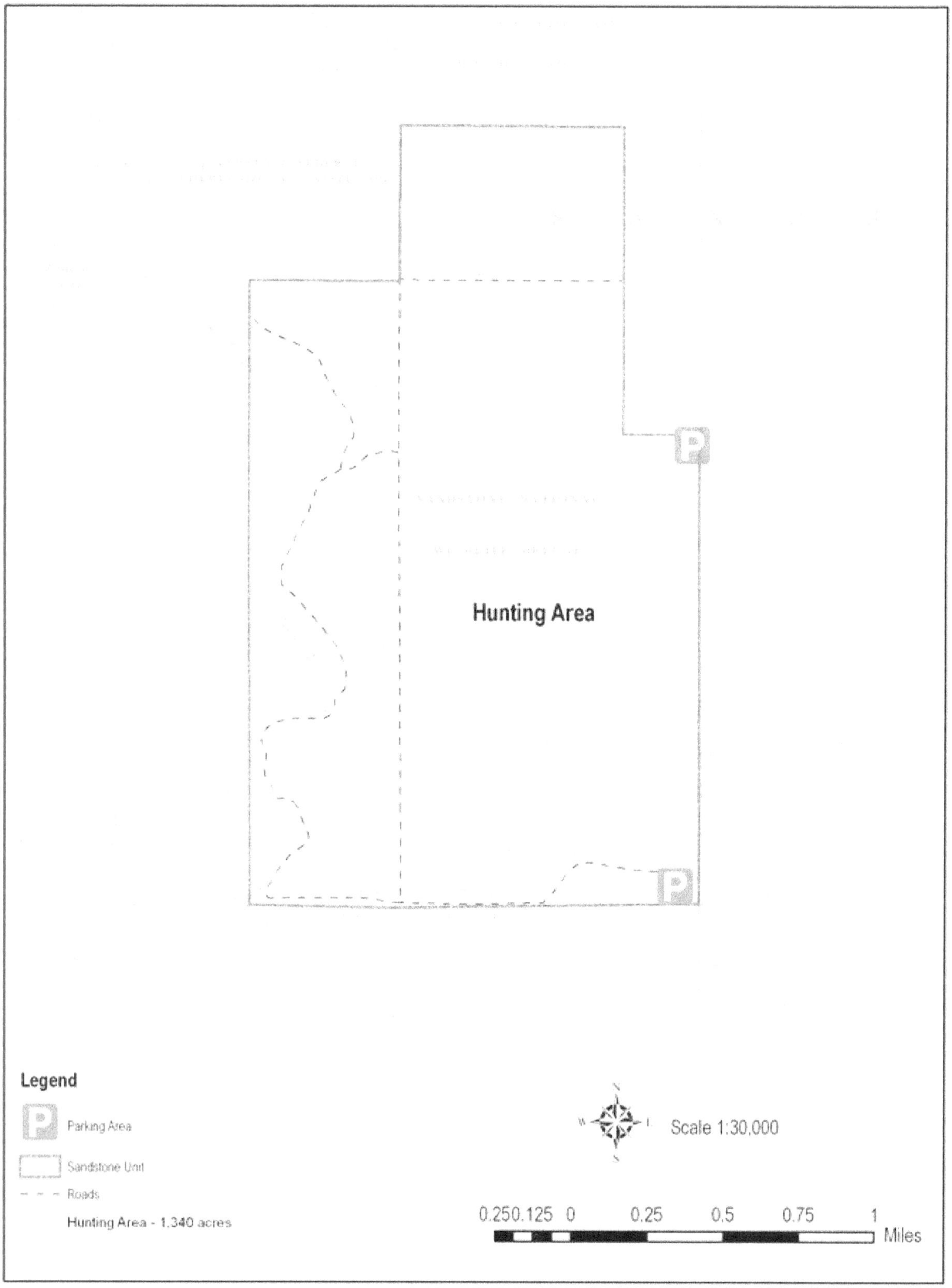

Hunting Area

Legend

P Parking Area

☐ Sandstone Unit

– – – Roads

Hunting Area - 1,340 acres

Scale 1:30,000

0.25 0.125 0   0.25   0.5   0.75   1   Miles

Strategies:

1. Upgrade and maintain the Refuge's website.

2. Regularly submit news articles to local newspapers.

3. Maintain regular contact with community leaders through presentations and conversations.

4. Continue participation in community events and celebrations.

5. Increase outreach efforts with local communities around the Sandstone Unit.

6. Hold annual special events on the Refuge (e.g. National Wildlife Refuge Week, International Migratory Bird Day, and Take a Kid Fishing).

7. Hire a park ranger/visitor services specialist.

Goal 4:

The American Indian community and the Refuge will preserve American Indian cultural values through communication, consultation, and cooperation.

Objective 4.1: American Indian Cultural Practices

Opportunities to engage in American Indian cultural practices will be available at the level offered in 2005.

Rationale: The Refuge is rich in both historic and pre-historic American Indian cultural traditions. Both the Dakota (Sioux) and Ojibwe (Chippewa) Indians used the resources of the lake and surrounding lands during historic times. Today, members of the Ojibwe Bands throughout northern Minnesota travel to the Refuge to practice rice harvesting using traditional methods. Members of the local East Lake Band also practice drumming ceremonies and maintain a cemetery on the Refuge.

Strategies:

1. Continue to coordinate with the local Ojibwe Bands for drumming ceremonies and burials.

2. Continue cooperating with the Ojibwe people for the harvest of wild rice on Rice Lake.

3. During the next 10 years follow biological objectives to ensure long-term wild rice production is sufficient to allow for a successful harvest an estimated 6 out of every 10 years. This strategy is linked to Objective 1.7; Strategy 2 and Objective 1.8; Strategy 3.

4. Consult with Ojibwe and Dakota peoples for interpretation and environmental education of American Indian history.

Objective 4.2: Archeological, Cultural, and Historic Protection

Over the life of the plan, avoid and protect or mitigate against disturbance of all known cultural, historic, or archeological sites.

Rationale: Cultural resources are an important facet of the country's heritage. Rice Lake NWR, like all national wildlife refuges, remains committed to preserving archeological and historic sites against degradation, looting, and other adverse impacts. The guiding principle for management derives from the *National Historic Preservation Act of 1966 as amended, 16 U.S.C. 470 et seq. and the Archeological Resources Protection Act of 1979 as amended, 16 U.S.C. 47011-mm*, which establish legal mandates and protection against identifying sites for the public, etc. The Refuge must ensure archeological and cultural values are described, identified, and taken into consideration prior to implementing undertakings. It is also essential that new site discoveries are documented. In order to meet these responsibilities, the Refuge intends to maintain an open dialogue with the Regional Historic Preservation Officer (RHPO) and to provide the RHPO with information about new archeological site discoveries. The Refuge will also cooperate with Federal, state, and local agencies, American Indian tribes, and the public in managing cultural resources on the Refuge.

Strategies:

1. Remove all buildings and facilities from Indian Point to avoid further degradation of this culturally important site (relocation site to be determined).

2. Conduct site-specific surveys prior to ground disturbing projects and protect known archeological, cultural and historic sites.

3. Within 10 years of CCP approval and with the assistance of the RHPO, develop a step-down plan for surveying lands to identify archeological resources and for developing a preservation program to meet the requirements of Section 14 of the Archaeological Resources Protection Act and Section 110(a)(2) of the National Historic Preservation Act.

4. Identify and nominate to the National Register of Historic Places all historic properties including those of religious and cultural significance to Indian tribes.

5. Inform the Regional Historic Preservation Officer early in project planning to ensure compliance with Section 106 of National Historic Preservation Act.

6. Contract with cultural resources firms specializing in Minnesota to conduct Phase I surveys prior to undertakings that could adversely affect historic resources.

7. In the event of inadvertent discoveries of ancient human remains, follow instructions and procedures indicated by the RHPO.

8. Ensure archeological and cultural values are described, identified, and taken into consideration prior to implementing undertakings.

9. Inspect the condition of known cultural resources on the Refuge and report to the RHPO changes in the conditions.

10. Integrate historic preservation with planning and management of other resources and activities.

11. Complete accessioning, cataloging, inventorying, and preserving the museum collection at the Refuge.

Goal 5:

Funding, staffing, facilities and public support will be sufficient to accomplish the purposes, vision, goals, and objectives of the Refuge.

Objective 5.1: Volunteer and Friends' Participation and Outside Assistance

Maintain volunteer participation, Friends' activities, and outside assistance at or above the 2005 level.

Rationale: With steady or declining budgets it is important for the Refuge to work closely with partners to secure alternative funding options and procure in-kind support for projects both on and off the Refuge. To have a functioning visitor services program it will be necessary to add a park ranger (visitor services specialist) to the Refuge. Visitor facilities on the Refuge need to be maintained at the current levels to ensure visitor security and provide adequate wildlife-dependent recreational opportunities. All facilities are and will be accessible according to ADA standards.

Additional facilities like pull-offs along the auto tour will need to be incorporated as Refuge visitation increases. All Refuge activities will benefit from volunteer participation, and certain activities will require volunteer participation to be successful. The Friends group needs to continue being an advocate of the Refuge and work with the Refuge to increase community awareness, secure funding through alternative sources, and assist with projects.

Strategies:

1. Strengthen the existing volunteer program and recruit new volunteers to assist with resource management and visitor services.

2. Ensure that Refuge office and maintenance needs are reflected in budget needs databases.

3. Support and encourage the Refuge Friends group to increase outreach and secure funding through grants and partnerships.

4. Continue to maintain Service-owned facilities using annual maintenance budget allocations.

5. Hire a park ranger (visitor services specialist) to increase outreach and develop a well-rounded visitor services program.

Mille Lacs National Wildlife Refuge

Goal 1: Goal

An optimum nesting population of Common Terns will exist on Hennepin Island and Refuge staff will know the productivity and chronology of species using Spirit Island.

Objective 1.1: Hennepin Island

Within 5 years of approval of the CCP, annually host a minimum of 150 nesting pairs and produce 100 fledglings annually upon completion of island enhancement.

Rationale: The Refuge contains one of four Common Tern breeding colonies in Minnesota. The Common Tern is currently listed by the State as a threatened species and has been named a resource conservation priority species for Region 3 by the U.S. Fish and Wildlife Service. It is also listed as high priority in all Bird Conservation Regions (BCRs) of Waterbird Plans. Since 1993,

Refuge staff annually construct a string grid over the southern one third of the island as a gull nesting deterrent but which still allows the Common Tern to pass through for nesting purposes. Assistance in maintaining the grid is provided by the Mille Lacs Band of Ojibwe's Department of Natural Resources. During the winter of 1996, 100 yards of pea-sized gravel were hauled to Hennepin Island as part of a habitat enhancement project. From 1998-2000, 100 fledglings or more were produced on the island annually, with the peak number of 200 fledging in 2000. Productivity has gone down since that time due to decreasing suitable nesting habitat, increasing water levels, erosion due to wave action and major storms decimating the colony in 2005. For the years 2003-2005, 51, 46, and 3 fledglings were produced respectively. An objective of producing 100 fledglings annually is challenging, but achievable with increased resources devoted to improving the conditions on the island.

Strategies:

1. Work with the Army Corps of Engineers to enlarge the island with gravel and construct rock jetties offshore to lessen erosion from wave action.

2. Maintain protective string grid above island.

3. Continue gull and Double-crested Cormorant control.

4. Continue to monitor Common Tern productivity.

Objective 1.2: Spirit Island

Annually estimate the productivity of birds on Spirit Island with scientifically credible data of known quality. The estimation will be able to detect at least a 20 percent change in productivity over 15 years.

Rationale: In order to understand and manage from a scientific foundation, basic data about wildlife use of the island is needed. Gathering sound data is a challenge because the island is remote from Refuge headquarters and wildlife use may be highly variable. Monitoring can be costly if high precision is sought. For this plan to succeed, an initial attempt to monitor birds should have the moderate goals specified in the objective, which will be achievable with available resources.

Strategies:

1. Develop and implement a monitoring plan for birds on Spirit Island.

Objective 1.3: Human Disturbance

Protect nesting birds and their habitat from human disturbance.

Rationale: The effects of human disturbance on nesting birds are well documented and are often profound. Depending on the timing and the degree of disturbance, birds may feel compelled to leave the nest temporarily or in some cases to abandon the nest permanently. Even a short-term departure during incubation or with young hatchlings can prove to be detrimental if it occurs during inclement weather or if avian predators are nearby. The issue of human disturbance is of greatest concern to the state-listed threatened Common Tern. In order to minimize impacts from human disturbance, Mille Lacs NWR will be closed to the public. Outreach and education at local marinas and public boat launches will be essential in reaching the fishing community and recreational boaters who use Mille Lacs Lake.

Strategies:

1. No public uses will be allowed.

2. Limit surveys and time of surveys.

3. Maintain boundary posting.

4. Provide periodic local updates on the status of the islands to satisfy local curiosity. Work with local resorts and the Minnesota DNR to disseminate information on restrictions.

Chapter 5: Plan Implementation

New and Existing Projects

This Comprehensive Conservation Plan calls for considerable staff commitment and funding to maintain and develop quality visitor facilities and wildlife habitat. The Refuge will need appropriate operations and maintenance funding to implement the strategies in this plan.

The following paragraphs describe the highest priority Refuge projects that will be implemented if staffing and funding allow.

Minimum Refuge Operations Needs

Provide funds to operate the Refuge office including expenses for heating, air conditioning, required safety inspections, electrical expenses, and safety improvements. These funds will also allow for upkeep of Refuge facilities including parking lots, interpretive kiosks, interpretive trails, and water control structures. It is important to provide a quality experience for the visitors who come to the Refuge each year. The project will help pay fuel bills, electric bills and the day-to-day costs of operating a refuge. (First year cost: $136,000, Recurring annual cost: $126,000)

Prepare a Forest Management Plan

Rice Lake NWR is in need of forestry expertise to produce a Forest Management Plan that is based on Refuge objectives and the 1997 Landscape Plan. The original forest management plan from 1984, though dated, contains excellent management guidelines for much of the Refuge forest. Forest fragmentation in northern Minnesota is a problem and an updated plan is imperative to proper management of the Refuge as well as assisting adjacent landowners with their management concerns. Preliminary inventory of forest types has been completed. Production of such a plan could be

Great Grey Owl, Rice Lake NWR

contracted if Service personnel with the required expertise are not available. (One-time cost: $70,000)

Private Lands/Refuge Biological Technician

An additional biologically trained staff member would enable a more intensive effort in Private Lands as well as contribute to on-Refuge habitat restoration and protection, provide assistance with surveys and censuses and provide better visitor services and outreach. The Refuge currently uses seasonal STEP students to fill this role. (First year cost: $118,000, Recurring annual cost: $53,000)

Increase Public Education and Outreach (Visitor Services Specialist)

Provide a visitor services specialist to respond to current and anticipated demand for visitor services and outreach. The Rice Lake Headquarters/Visitor

Center is located along a major highway that leads tourists to the central Minnesota lakes, Duluth, and Lake Superior north shore areas. Highway signs direct visitors to the Refuge and have helped to increase visitation by over 50 percent in the last few years. Interpretation/education/outreach will be paramount to the continued public support of the Refuge System. A visitor services specialist position would fill a demand for professional wildlife-dependent recreation programs and opportunities, provide programs on Service activities, and produce news releases. This would also allow weekend visitor contacts, increased coordination with our Friends Group, and increased volunteer recruitment and retention. (First year cost: $71,000, Recurring annual cost: $45,000)

Prepare a Cultural Resources Management Plan

Contract with a cultural resources professional to complete a cultural resources management plan. The plan would include the Section 14 and Section 110(a)(2) surveys and analysis of all cultural resources including pre-historic and historic wild ricing locations by Indians and Euro-American inhabitants, early Refuge facilities such as dams, water control structures, and CCC activities, as well as a determination of whether any significant conservation or wildlife activities occurred on the Refuge. An element of the cultural resources survey will be to examine the past and present impacts to the culturally sensitive area known as Indian Point. A detailed survey and analysis of Indian Point will be essential in determining the effects of building removal. Additional upland areas adjacent to the Wildlife Drive and Highway 65 will also need a detailed survey and analysis to assist in determining the effects of constructing new buildings. (One-time cost: $60,000)

Expand Wildlife Observation and Interpretation Opportunities on Refuge

Provide accessible towers, viewing scopes, interpretive signs, auto tour guide, orientation kiosk and trailhead signs to improve services for visitors. The Rice Lake NWR Office is located along a major highway that leads tourists to the central Minnesota lakes, Duluth, and Lake Superior north shore areas. Highway signs direct visitors to the Refuge and have helped to increase visitation by over 50 percent in the last few years. Interpretive facilities will allow the Refuge to educate the public about Rice Lake NWR, a Globally Important Bird Area that hosts up to one million Ring-necked Ducks during fall migration. (One-time cost: $97,000)

Increase Management Capability with a GIS / GPS System (Biological Technician)

Management of habitats on Rice Lake NWR would be enhanced by the computer technology of a Geographic Information System supported by a Global Positioning System. Purchase of this system, addition of a Biological Technician and the development of forest inventory, vegetation classification, soil mapping and overlays of human and cultural resources will lead to best long-term management decisions and long-term health of the ecosystem. (First year cost: $104,000, Recurring annual cost: $53,000)

Remove/Relocate all Buildings and Facilities from Indian Point

Conduct cultural resource surveys on sites located near State Highway 65 that have suitable soils, sufficient size to accommodate the relocation of all Refuge maintenance facilities and housing requirements, and not significantly add to habitat fragmentation concerns. Removal of all buildings from Indian Point will eliminate further degradation of this important cultural site due to future new con-

Rice Lake NWR

Table 4: Existing Staff and Proposal Additional Staff, Rice Lake NWR

Position	Existing	Proposed New
Refuge Manager	1 FTE	
Park Ranger/Visitor Services	1 FTE vacant	
Refuge Operations Specialist		1 FTE
Biologist	1 FTE	
Biological Technician		1 FTE
Biological Technician	0.6 FTE	0.1 FTE
Park Ranger/Visitor Services		0.6 FTE
Administrative Technician	1 FTE	
Maintenance Mechanic	1 FTE	
Maintenance Mechanic	.75 FTE	0.25 FTE

struction and expansion requirements. The present age and condition for several of the buildings will soon require new construction:

- Quarters No. 2 was constructed in 1941 and has a basement wall that is buckling.

- The six-stall garage has no electrical service.

- The quonset storage building built in 1956 is in serious decay.

- The three-stall garage/bunkhouse was built in 1952 and fails to meet Service standards for health and safety. (One-time cost: $3.9 million.)

Future Staffing Requirements

In order for the Refuge to be fully successful in completing the strategies of the goals and objectives in the Comprehensive Conservation Plan and the priority RONS projects, the positions noted in Table 4 are considered essential future staffing requirements.

This staffing plan requires 9.3 full-time employees, compared to the 6.35 FTEs currently approved for the Refuge. While 6.35 FTEs may be the approved staffing level, there is currently a vacancy that is unfilled due to steady or declining budgets within the National Wildlife Refuge System. The position will, unfortunately, remain vacant for an undetermined length of time.

Existing hiring programs will be looked at as a way to provide employment opportunities to qualified Mille Lacs Band of Ojibwe/American Indian youth (e.g. Student Career Enhancement Program).

Partnership Opportunities

Partnerships are essential to the successful implementation of this CCP. We plan to foster existing partnerships and develop new ones when opportunities arise. The Minnesota DNR will continue to be an important partner in bog management on approximately 8,000 contiguous acres along the Refuge's north border. The Aitkin County Land Department will be an important partner in developing forest management objectives along the Refuge's south border. The Mille Lacs Band of Ojibwe will continue to be an important partner in the management of Mille Lacs NWR. The Refuge staff will continue to contribute expertise and other resources, where possible, to individuals and groups requesting assistance with activities beneficial to Service trust resources.

The Refuge's volunteer program will be vital to the fulfillment of the Refuge vision. Volunteers will continue to assist the Refuge in nearly every aspect of its operation. We expect the special partnership with the Friends of Rice Lake Refuge to flourish and bring the Refuge and community closer together.

Step-down Management Plans

Step-down management plans help meet the goals and objectives of the CCP. Some step-down plans are required by Service policy and others are used to specify strategies and implementation schedules beyond the detail of the CCP. The following list shows the step-down management plans we intend to prepare or revise to realize the intent of the CCP.

The Habitat Management Plan, Visitor Services Plan, and Inventory and Monitoring Plan are essential to describe forest management, wildlife-dependent recreation programs, and credible evaluation of management. The Fire Management Plan, approved in 2002 and revised every 5 years, provides direction and establishes procedures to guide various wildland fire program activities. The Fire Management Plan covers the historical and ecological role of fire, fire management objectives, preparedness, suppression, fire management actions and responses, fire impacts, use of prescribed fire, and fire management restrictions.

Table 5: Step-down Management Plans, Rice Lake NWR

Step-down Management Plan and Subplans	Plan Date Completed/ Updated	Anticipated Completion/ Revision [1]
Habitat Management Plan	1997 (Landscape Plan)	2008
Marsh and Water Management Plan	1981	
Forest Management Plan	1984	
Grassland Management Plan	1989 (Cropland Management Plan)	
Visitor Services Plan	New	2009
Hunting Plan	1990	
Fishery Management Plan	1987	
Law Enforcement Plan	1987	
Accessibility Plan	New	
Visit Quality Monitoring Plan	New	
Wildlife and Habitat Inventory and Monitoring Plan	1996	2008
Fire Management Plan	2002	2008
Cultural Resources Management Plan	New	2010
Museum Property Inventory and Scope Statement	New	
Furbearer Management Plan	2000	2009
Trapping Plan	Annual	

1.*Includes all subplans.*

Monitoring and Evaluation

Monitoring is critical to successful implementation of this plan. Monitoring is necessary to evaluate the progress toward objectives and to determine if conditions are changing.

Accomplishment of the objectives described in this CCP will be monitored annually by the Refuge Manager and his or her supervisor. The public will be informed about the activities of the Refuge staff through periodic mailings to persons on the mailing list and published on the Refuge website. The tech-niques and details for monitoring related to specific objectives will be specified in the Inventory and Monitoring Step-down Plan.

The direction set forth in this CCP and specifically identified strategies and projects will be monitored throughout the life of this plan. Periodically, the Regional Office will assemble a station review team to visit the Refuge and evaluate current Refuge activities in light of this plan. The team will review all aspects of Refuge management, including direction, accomplishments and funding. The goals and objectives presented in this CCP will provide the baseline from which this field station will be evaluated.

Archeological and Cultural Values

As part of its larger conservation mandate and ethic, the Service, through the Refuge Manager, applies historic preservation laws and regulations to ensure historic properties are identified and are protected to the extent possible within its established purposes and Refuge System mission.

The Refuge Manager early in project planning for all undertakings, informs the RHPO (Regional Historic Preservation Officer) to initiate the Section 106 process. Concurrent with public notification and involvement for environmental compliance and compatibility determinations if applicable, or cultural resources only if no other issues are involved, the Refuge Manager informs and requests comments from the public and local officials through presentations, meetings, and media notices; results are provided to the RHPO.

Archeological investigations and collecting are performed only in the public interest by qualified archeologists or by persons recommended by the Governor working under an Archaeological Resources Protection Act permit issued by the Regional Director. In addition, the Refuge Manager has found this third-party use of Refuge land to be compatible, (The requirements of ARPA apply to Service cultural resources contracts as well: the contract is the equivalent of a permit.) and issues a special use permit. Refuge personnel take steps to prevent unauthorized collecting by the public, contractors, and Refuge personnel; violators are cited or other appropriate action taken. Violations are reported to the Regional Historic Preservation Officer.

The Refuge Manager will, with the assistance of the RHPO, develop a step-down plan for surveying lands to identify archeological resources and for developing a preservation program to meet the requirements of Section 14 of the Archaeological Resources Protection Act and Section 110(a)(2) of the National Historic Preservation Act.

The Refuge Manager should have and implement a plan for inspecting the condition of known cultural resources on the Refuge and report to the RHPO changes in the conditions.

The Refuge Manager will initiate budget requests or otherwise obtain funding from the 1 percent Operations and Maintenance program base provided for the Section 106 process compliance:

1. Inventory, evaluate, and protect all significant cultural resources located on lands controlled by the FWS, including historic properties of religious and cultural significance to Indian tribes.

2. Identify and nominate to the National Register of Historic Places all historic properties including those of religious and cultural significance to Indian tribes.

3. Cooperate with Federal, state, and local agencies, American Indian tribes, and the public in managing cultural resources on the Refuge.

4. Integrate historic preservation with planning and management of other resources and activities. Historic buildings are rehabilitated and adapted to reuse when feasible.

5. Recognize the rights of American Indian to have access to certain religious sites and objects on Refuge lands within the limitations of the NWRS mission.

Plan Review and Revision

The CCP is meant to provide guidance to the Refuge manager and staff over the next 15 years. However, the CCP is also a dynamic and flexible document and several of the strategies contained in the plan are subject to natural, uncontrollable events such as windstorms and droughts. Likewise, many of the strategies are dependent upon Service funding for staff and projects. Finally, the CCP was developed using the best information available at the time of preparation. As new and better information emerges, the direction and strategies of the CCP may need to be re-evaluated. Because of these factors, the recommendations in the CCP will be reviewed periodically and, if necessary, revised to meet new circumstances. If any revisions are major, the review and revision will include the public.

Appendix A: Finding of No Significant Impact

Finding of No Significant Impact

Environmental Assessment and Comprehensive Conservation Plan for Rice Lake and Mille Lacs National Wildlife Refuges, Minnesota

An Environmental Assessment (EA) has been prepared to identify management strategies to meet the conservation goals of the Rice Lake and Mille Lacs National Wildlife Refuges (NWRs). The EA examined the environmental consequences that each management alternative could have on the quality of the physical, biological, and human environment, as required by the National Environmental Policy Act of 1969 (NEPA). The EA evaluated two alternatives for the future management of the Refuges.

The alternative selected for implementation on each refuge is *Alternative B*. The preferred alternative for Rice Lake NWR includes improving the long-term sustainability of wild rice in Rice Lake; reestablishing the white pine super-canopy in Refuge forests; and strengthening programs in wildlife-dependent recreation and cultural resources protection. Native American access to the Refuge for harvesting of wild rice and ceremonies will continue. The preferred alternative for Mille Lacs NWR includes reversing the erosion of Hennepin Island through rebuilding and protection with a constructed reef. The island will continue to provide for a nesting colony for the State-listed threatened Common Tern.

For reasons presented above and below, and based on an evaluation of the information contained in the Environmental Assessment, we have determined that the action of adopting Alternative B as the management alternative for each refuge is not a major federal action which would significantly affect the quality of the human environment, within the meaning of Section 102 (2) (c) of the National Environmental Policy Act of 1969.

Additional Reasons:

1. Future management actions will have a neutral or positive impact on the local economy.
2. This action will not have an adverse impact on threatened or endangered species.

Supporting References:

Environmental Assessment
Comprehensive Conservation Plan

ACTING Regional Director   12/4/07
                                     Date

Appendix B: Glossary

Appendix B: Glossary

Alternative

A set of objectives and strategies needed to achieve refuge goals and the desired future condition.

Biological Diversity

The variety of life forms and its processes, including the variety of living organisms, the genetic differences among them, and the communities and ecosystems in which they occur.

Compatible Use

A wildlife-dependent recreational use, or any other use on a refuge that will not materially interfere with or detract from the fulfillment of the mission of the Service or the purposes of the refuge.

Comprehensive Conservation Plan

A document that describes the desired future conditions of the refuge, and specifies management actions to achieve refuge goals and the mission of the National Wildlife Refuge System.

Cultural Resources

"Those parts of the physical environment -- natural and built -- that have cultural value to some kind of sociocultural group ... [and] those nonmaterial human social institutions...." Cultural resources include historic sites, archeological sites and associated artifacts, sacred sites, traditional cultural properties, cultural items (human remains, funerary objects, sacred objects, and objects of cultural patrimony), and buildings and structures.

Ecosystem

A dynamic and interrelated complex of plant and animal communities and their associated non-living environment.

Ecosystem Approach

A strategy or plan to protect and restore the natural function, structure, and species composition of an ecosystem, recognizing that all components are interrelated.

Ecosystem Management

Management of an ecosystem that includes all ecological, social and economic components that make up the whole of the system.

Endangered Species

Any species of plant or animal defined through the Endangered Species Act as being in danger of extinction throughout all or a significant portion of its range, and published in the Federal Register.

Environmental Assessment

A systematic analysis to determine if proposed actions would result in a significant effect on the quality of the environment.

Extirpation

The local extinction of a species that is no longer found in a locality or country, but exists elsewhere in the world.

Goals

Descriptive statements of desired future conditions.

Interjurisdictional Fish

Fish that occur in waters under the jurisdiction of one or more states, for which there is an interstate fishery management plan or which migrates between the waters under the jurisdiction of two or more states bordering on the Great Lakes.

Issue

Any unsettled matter that requires a management decision. For example, a resource management problem, concern, a threat to natural resources, a conflict in uses, or in the presence of an undesirable resource condition.

National Wildlife Refuge System

All lands, waters, and interests therein administered by the U.S. Fish and Wildlife Service as wildlife refuges, wildlife ranges, wildlife management areas, waterfowl production areas, and other areas for the protection and conservation of fish, wildlife and plant resources.

Objectives

A concise statement of what we want to achieve. The statement is specific, measurable, achievable, results oriented, and time-fixed.

Preferred Alternative

The Service's selected alternative identified in the environmental assessment and fully developed in the Comprehensive Conservation Plan.

Scoping

A process for determining the scope of issues to be addressed by a comprehensive conservation plan and for identifying the significant issues. Involved in the scoping process are federal, state and local agencies; private organizations; and individuals.

Species

A distinctive kind of plant or animal having distinguishable characteristics, and that can interbreed and produce young. A category of biological classification.

Strategies

A general approach or specific actions to achieve objectives.

Threatened Species

Those plant or animal species likely to become endangered species throughout all of or a significant portion of their range within the foreseeable future. A plant or animal identified and defined in accordance with the 1973 Endangered Species Act and published in the Federal Register.

Undertaking:

"A project, activity, or program funded in whole or in part under the direct or indirect jurisdiction of a Federal agency, including those carried out by or on behalf of a Federal agency; those carried out with Federal financial assistance; those requiring a Federal permit, license or approval...," i.e., all Federal actions.

Vegetation

Plants in general, or the sum total of the plant life in an area.

Vegetation Type

A category of land based on potential or existing dominant plant species of a particular area.

Watershed

The entire land area that collects and drains water into a stream or stream system.

Wetland

Areas such as lakes, marshes, and streams that are inundated by surface or ground water for a long enough period of time each year to support, and that do support under natural conditions, plants and animals that require saturated or seasonally saturated soils.

Wildlife-dependent Recreational Use

A use of refuge that involves hunting, fishing, wildlife observation and photography, or environmental education and interpretation, as identified in the National Wildlife Refuge System Improvement Act of 1997.

Wildlife Diversity

A measure of the number of wildlife species in an area.

Water Birds

This general category includes all birds that inhabit lakes, marshes, streams and other wetlands at some point during the year. The group includes all waterfowl, such as ducks, geese, and swans, and other birds such as loons, rails, cranes, herons, egrets, ibis, cormorants, pelicans, shorebirds and passerines that nest and rely on wetland vegetation.

Appendix C: Wildlife Species of Concern

Appendix C: Wildlife Species of Concern

The U.S. Fish & Wildlife Region 3 Resource Conservation Priorities, 2002, identify the species considered to be in the greatest need of attention under the Service's full span of authorities, including the conservation, protection, and recovery of migratory birds, threatened and endangered species, interjurisdictional fish, and control of nuisance species. The species shown below are priorities for the Mississippi Headwaters/Tallgrass Prairie Ecosystem, which contains Rice Lake and Mille Lacs NWRs.

The Minnesota's 2006 Comprehensive Conservation Strategy identified species with the greatest conservation need in the Mille Lacs Uplands, St. Louis Moraines, and Tamarack Lowlands subsections, which contain Rice Lake and Mille Lakes NWRs (Figure 6).

The species in the following table are a subset of the two lists that are expected to benefit from Refuge management.

Common Name	Status Classification	Concerns	RCP	SGCN*
MAMMALS				
American Badger				M
Canada Lynx	Federal Endangered/State Special Concern			M, S
Eastern Spotted Skunk	State Threatened			M, S, T
Franklin's Ground Squirrel				M, S, T
Gray Wolf	State Special Concern	Recovering Species, Tribal trust	x	M, S, T
Least Weasel	State Special Concern			M
Northern Bog Lemming	State Special Concern			S
BIRDS				
American Avocet				M
American Bittern		Rare/declining	x	M, S, T
American Black Duck				S, T
American Golden-plover				M, S, T
American Woodcock		Recreational/economic value, Rare/declining	x	M, S, T
Bald Eagle	Federal Threatened/State Special Concern	Proposed Rule (Delist from ESA), Tribal trust	x	M, S, T
Black Tern		Rare/declining	x	M, S, T
Black-backed Woodpecker				M, S, T
Black-billed Cuckoo		Rare/declining	x	M, S, T
Black-crowned Night-Heron		Rare/declining	x	
Blue-winged Teal		Recreational/economic value	x	
Bobolink		Rare/declining	x	M
Boreal Chickadee				S, T
Brown Thrasher				M, S, T
Buff-breasted Sandpiper		Rare/declining	x	M, S, T
Canada Goose – Migrant Populations		Recreational/economic value	x	
Canada Goose – Resident Population (Giants & Urban Giants)		Recreational/economic value, "Nuisance"	x	

Common Name	Status Classification	Concerns	RCP	SGCN*
Canada Warbler		Rare/declining	x	M, S, T
Canvasback		Recreational/economic value	x	
Cape May Warbler				M, T
Cerulean Warbler	State Special Concern			M
Common Loon		Rare/declining	x	M, S, T
Common Nighthawk				M, S, T
Common Tern – Great Lakes Population	State Threatened	Rare/declining	x	M
Connecticut Warbler		Rare/declining	x	M, S, T
Dickcissel		Rare/declining	x	
Double-crested Cormorant		"Nuisance"	x	
Dunlin				M, S, T
Eastern Meadowlark		Rare/declining	x	M
Eastern Wood-pewee				M, S, T
Field Sparrow		Rare/declining	x	M
Forster's Tern	State Special Concern	Rare/declining	x	M
Golden-winged Warbler		Rare/declining	x	M, S, T
Grasshopper Sparrow		Rare/declining	x	M
Greater Yellowlegs		Rare/declining	x	M, S, T
Henslow's Sparrow		Rare/declining	x	
Hudsonian Godwit		Rare/declining	x	M
Least Bittern		Rare/declining	x	M
Least Flycatcher				M, S, T
LeConte's Sparrow		Rare/declining	x	M, S, T
Lesser Scaup		Recreational/economic value, Rare/declining	x	
Long-eared Owl		Rare/declining	x	
Mallard		Recreational/economic value	x	
Marbled Godwit	State Special Concern	Rare/declining	x	
Marsh Wren				M, S, T
Nelson's Sharp-tailed Sparrow	State Special Concern	Rare/declining	x	M, S
Northern Flicker		Rare/declining	x	
Northern Goshawk		Rare/declining	x	M, S, T
Northern Harrier		Rare/declining	x	M, S, T
Northern Pintail		Recreational/economic value, Rare/declining	x	
Northern Rough-winged Swallow				M, S, T
Olive-sided Flycatcher		Rare/declining	x	M, S, T
Orchard Oriole		Rare/declining	x	
Ovenbird				M, S, T
Peregrine Falcon	State Threatened	Rare/declining, ESA Delisted, Recreational/economic value	x	
Red-headed Woodpecker		Rare/declining	x	M, S, T

Common Name	Status Classification	Concerns	RCP	SGCN*
Red-necked Grebe				M, S, T
Red-shouldered Hawk	State Special Concern	Rare/declining	x	M, S
Rose-breasted Grosbeak				M, S, T
Ruddy Turnstone				M, S
Sedge Wren		Rare/declining	x	M, S, T
Semipalmated Sandpiper				M, S, T
Sharp-tailed Grouse				M
Short-billed Dowitcher		Rare/declining	x	M, S, T
Short-eared Owl		Rare/declining	x	T
Snow Goose		Recreational/economic value, "Nuisance"	x	
Stilt Sandpiper		Rare/declining	x	
Swamp Sparrow				M, S, T
Trumpeter Swan	State Threatened	Rare/declining, Recreational/ economic value	x	M, S, T
Upland Sandpiper		Rare/declining	x	M
Veery				M, S, T
Virginia Rail				M, S, T
Western Meadowlark		Rare/declining	x	
Whimbrel		Rare/declining	x	M, S
Whip-poor-will		Rare/declining	x	M, S, T
White-rumped Sandpiper				M, S
White-throated Sparrow				M, S, T
Willow Flycatcher				M
Wilson's Phalarope	State Threatened	Rare/declining	x	T
Winter Wren				M, S, T
Wood Duck		Recreational/economic value	x	
Wood Thrush		Rare/declining	x	M, S, T
Yellow Rail	State Special Concern	Rare/declining	x	M, S, T
Yellow-bellied Sapsucker				M, S, T
REPTILES and AMPHIBIANS				
Blanding's Turtle	State Threatened			M
Common Mudpuppy				M
Common Snapping Turtle	State Special Concern			M, S, T
Eastern Hognose Snake				M
Eastern Red-backed Salamander				S, T
Four-toed Salamander	State Special Concern			S
Spotted Salamander				M
Wood Turtle	State Threatened			M, T
FISH				
Gilt Darter	State Special Concern			M
Greater Redhorse				M, T

Common Name	Status Classification	Concerns	RCP	SGCN*
Lake Sturgeon – Inland population	State Special Concern	Rare/declining, Recreational/ economic value, Tribal trust	x	M, S, T
Largescale Stoneroller				M
Least Darter				M
Longear Sunfish				M
Northern Brook Lamprey	State Special Concern			M
Pugnose Shiner	State Special Concern			M
Southern Brook Lamprey	State Special Concern			M
INSECTS and SPIDERS				
A Caddisfly (6 species)	State Special Concern			M, S
A Jumping Spider (2 species)	State Special Concern			M, S, T
A Tiger Beetle	State Special Concern			M
Bog Copper				M, S, T
Disa Alpine	State Special Concern			T
Green-faced Clubtail				M
Grizzled Skipper	State Special Concern			S, T
Leonard's Skipper	State Special Concern			M
Macoun's Arctic				M, S, T
Persius Duskywing	State Endangered			M
Polycentropus milaca (caddisfly)	State Special Concern			S
Pygmy Snaketail				M
Skillet Clubtail				M
St. Croix Snaketail	State Special Concern			M
Tawny Crescent				M, S, T
Two-spotted Skipper				M
Vertrees's Ceraclean Caddisfly	State Special Concern			M
MOLLUSKS				
Black Sandshell	State Special Concern	Rare/declining (range overlaps commercial harvested areas)	x	M, S, T
Creek Heelsplitter	State Special Concern			M, S, T
Elktoe	State Threatened	Rare/declining (range overlaps commercial harvested areas)	x	M
Hickorynut	State Special Concern			M
Mucket Mussel	State Threatened			M
Purple Wartyback	State Threatened			M
Round Pigtoe	State Threatened	Rare/declining (range overlaps commercial harvested areas)	x	M
Snail (4 species)		Rare/declining (status assessment underway)	x	
Spectaclecase	State Threatened			M
Spike	State Special Concern			M
Threeridge		Recreational/economic value	x	
Zebra Mussel		"Nuisance"	x	

Common Name	Status Classification	Concerns	RCP	SGCN*
CRUSTACEANS				
Rusty Crayfish		"Nuisance"	x	
*Species with the greatest conservation need (SGCN) subsections: M, Mille Lacs Uplands S, St. Louis Moraines T, Tamarack Lowlands				

Appendix D: Species Lists

Mammal Species List for Rice Lake NWR

Scientific Name	Common Name	Source	Confirmed	Date	Confirmed by
DIDELPHIMORPHA: Didelphidae					
Didelphis virginiana	Virginia opossum	Burt 1976			
INSECTIVORA: Soricidae					
Sorex arcticus	Arctic shrew	Burt 1976	V	2001	MNCBS
Sorex cinereus	Cinereus shrew	Burt 1976	V	2001	MNCBS
Sorex hoyi	Pygmy shrew	Burt 1976	V	2001	MNCBS
Sorex palustris	Common water shrew	Burt 1976			
Blarina brevicauda	Northern short-tailed shrew	Burt 1976	V	2001	MNCBS
INSECTIVORA: Talpidae					
Condylura cristata	Star-nosed mole	Burt 1976			
CHIROPTERA: Vespertilionidae					
Myotis lucifugus	Little brown myotis	Burt 1976	F	2001	MNCBS
Myotis septentrionalis	Northern myotis	Burt 1976			
Lasiurus borealis	Eastern red bat	Burt 1976			
Lasiurus cinereus	Hoary bat	Burt 1976			
Lasionycteris noctivagans	Silver-haired bat	Burt 1976	F	2001	MNCBS
Pipistrellus subflavus	Eastern pipistelle	Burt 1976			
Eptesicus fuscus	Big brown bat	Burt 1976	F	2001	MNCBS
CARNIVORA: Canidae					
Canis latrans	Coyote	Burt 1976	T	2001	MNCBS
Canis lupus	Gray wolf	Burt 1976	T	2001	MNCBS
Vulpes vulpes	Red fox	Burt 1976	T	2001	MNCBS
Urocyon cinereoargenteus	Common gray fox	Burt 1976	O	1998	D. Huhta
CARNIVORA: Ursidae					
Ursus americanus	Black bear	Burt 1976	O	2001	MNCBS
CARNIVORA: Procyonidae					
Procyon lotor	Common raccoon	Burt 1976	T	2001	MNCBS
CARNIVORA: Mustelidae					
Martes americana	American marten		O	early 1990's	D. Huhta
Martes pennanti	Fisher		O	8/1/02	M. McDowell
Mustela erminea	Ermine	Burt 1976	V	2001	MNCBS
Mustela frenata	Long-tailed weasel	Burt 1976			
Mustela nivalis	Least weasel	Burt 1976			
Mustela vison	American mink	Burt 1976	O	1998	D. Huhta
Taxidea taxus	American badger	Burt 1976	O	late 1980's	D. Huhta
Lutra canadensis	Northern river otter	Burt 1976	O	2001	MNCBS
Spilogale putorius	Eastern spotted skunk	Burt 1976			
Mephitis mephitis	Striped skunk	Burt 1976	V	2001	MNCBS
CARNIVORA: Felidae					
Felis concolor	Mountain lion	Burt 1976	O	1991	D. Huhta

Mammal Species List for Rice Lake NWR (Continued)

Scientific Name	Common Name	Source	Confirmed	Date	Confirmed by
Lynx canadensis	Canada lynx	Burt 1976	O	3/17/06	D. Huhta & C. DeMenge
Lynx rufus	Bobcat	Burt 1976	O	9/2/03	M. McDowell
ARTIODACTYLA: Cervidae					
Cervus elaphus	Elk*				
Odocoileus hemionus	Mule deer	Burt 1976			
Odocoileus virginianus	White-tailed deer	Burt 1976	O	2001	MNCBS
Alces alces	Moose		O	6/24/06	C. DeMenge
Rangifer tarandus	Caribou*				
ARTIODACTYLA: Bovidae					
Bos bison	American bison*				
RODENTIA: Sciuridae					
Tamias minimus	Least chipmunk	Burt 1976			
Tamias striatus	Eastern chipmunk	Burt 1976	O	2001	MNCBS
Marmota monax	Woodchuck	Burt 1976	O	2003	M. McDowell
Spermophilus franklinii	Franklin's ground squirrel	Burt 1976	V	2001	MNCBS
Spermophilus tridecemlineatus	Thirteen-lined ground squirrel	Burt 1976			
Sciurus carolinensis	Eastern gray squirrel	Burt 1976	O	2001	MNCBS
Sciurus niger	Eastern fox squirrel	Burt 1976			
Tamiasciurus hudsonicus	Red squirrel	Burt 1976	O	2001	MNCBS
Glaucomys sabrinus	Northern flying squirrel	Burt 1976	O	Nov-06	M. McDowell
Glaucomys volans	Southern flying squirrel	Burt 1976			
RODENTIA: Geomyidae					
Geomys bursarius	Plains pocket gopher	Burt 1976	T	2001	MNCBS
RODENTIA: Castoridae					
Castor canadensis	American beaver	Burt 1976	O	2001	MNCBS
RODENTIA: Muridae (Cricetinae)					
Peromyscus leucopus	White-footed mouse	Burt 1976	V	2001	MNCBS
Peromyscus maniculatus gracilis	Woodland deer mouse	Burt 1976	V	2001	MNCBS
RODENTIA: Muridae (Arvicolinae)					
Clethrionomys gapperi	Southern red-backed vole	Burt 1976	V	2001	MNCBS
Microtus pennsylvanicus	Meadow vole	Burt 1976	V	2001	MNCBS
Ondatra zibethicus	Common muskrat	Burt 1976	O	2003	M. McDowell
Synaptomys cooperi	Southern bog lemming	Burt 1976	V	2001	MNCBS
RODENTIA: Dipodidae (Zapodinae)					
Zapus hudsonius	Meadow jumping mouse	Burt 1976	V	2001	MNCBS
Napaeozapus insignis	Woodland jumping mouse	Burt 1976			
RODENTIA: Erethizontidae					
Erethizon dorsatum	Common porcupine	Burt 1976	T	2001	MNCBS
LAGOMORPHA: Leporidae					

Mammal Species List for Rice Lake NWR (Continued)

Scientific Name	Common Name	Source	Confirmed	Date	Confirmed by
Sylvilagus floridanus	Eastern cottontail	Burt 1976	O	2004	M. McDowell
Lepus americanus	Snowshoe hare	Burt 1976	T	2001	MNCBS

V = voucher specimen, P = photo, F = call file, C = capture/release
O = observation, S = sound or vocalization, T = tracks or sign
MNCBS = Minnesota County Biological Survey, Minnesota Department of Natural Resources
*extirpated species
Source: W. Burt, R. Grossenheider. 1976. A field guide to the mammals of North America. Peterson Field Guide Series. Houghton Mifflin Company. New York, New York. 289 pages.

Butterfly and Moth Species List, Rice Lake NWR

Species		
Scientific Name	Common Name	Source
Calopteryx maculata	Ebony Jewelwing	Stokes
Celithemis elisa	Calico Pennant	Dunkle
Celithemis eponina	Halloween Pennant	Dunkle
Tramea lacerata	Black Saddlebags	Dunkle
Perithemis tenera	Eastern Amberwing	Dunkle
Neurocordulia yamaskanensis	Stygian Shadowdragon	Dunkle
Somatochlora franklini	Delicate Emerald	Dunkle
Somatochlora kennedyi	Kennedy's Emerald	Dunkle
Somatochlora forcipata	Forcipate Emerald	Dunkle
Somatochlora ensigera	Plains Emerald	Dunkle
Somatochlora walshii	Brush-tipped Emerald	Dunkle
Somatochlora minor	Ocellated Emerald	Dunkle
Somatochlora elongata	Ski-Tailed Emerald	Dunkle
Somatochlora williamsoni	Williamson's Emerald	Dunkle
Epitheca cynosura	Common Baskettail	Dunkle
Epitheca princeps	Prince Baskettail	Dunkle
Williamsonia fletcheri	Ebony Boghaunter	Dunkle
Dorocordulia libera	Racket-Tailed Emerald	Dunkle
Macromia illinoiensis	Illinois River Cruiser	Dunkle
Didymops transversa	Stream Cruiser	Dunkle
Cordulegaster maculata	Twin-Spotted Spiketail	Dunkle
Arigomphus cornutus	Horned Clubtail	Dunkle
Arigomphus furcifer	Lilypad Clubtail	Dunkle

Butterfly and Moth Species List, Rice Lake NWR (Continued)

Species		
Scientific Name	**Common Name**	**Source**
Dromogomphus spinosus	Black-Shouldered Spinyleg	Dunkle
Stylurus notatus	Elusive Clubtail	Dunkle
Stylurus amnicola	Riverine Clubtail	Dunkle
Stylurus spiniceps	Arrow Clubtail	Dunkle
Gomphus externus	Plains Clubtail	Dunkle
Gomphus fraternus	Midland Clubtail	Dunkle
Gomphus lineatifrons	Splendid Clubtail	Dunkle
Gomphus vastus	Cobra Clubtail	Dunkle
Gomphus ventricosus	Skillet Clubtail	Dunkle
Gomphus viridifrons	Green-Faced Clubtail	Dunkle
Gomphus adelphus	Mustached Clubtail	Dunkle
Gomphus exilis	Lancet Clubtail	Dunkle
Gomphus Spicatus	Dusky Clubtail	Dunkle
Gomphus lividus	Ashy Clubtail	Dunkle
Gomphus quadricolor	Rapids Clubtail	Dunkle
Gomphus graslinellus	Pronghorn Clubtail	Dunkle
Oplonaeschna armata	Riffle Darner	Dunkle
Aeshna sitchensis	Zigzag Darner	Dunkle
Aeshna verticalis	Green-Striped Darner	Dunkle
Aeshna tuberculifera	Black-Tipped Darner	Dunkle
Aeshna eremita	Lake Darner	Dunkle
Aeshna constricta	Lance-Tipped Darner	Dunkle
Boyeria grafiana	Ocellated Darner	Dunkle
Calopteryx aequabilis	River Jewelwing	Stokes
Lestes disjunctus	Common Spreadwing	Stokes
Lestes congener	Spotted Spreadwing	Stokes
Lestes dryas	Emerald Spreadwing	Stokes
Lestes rectangularis	Slender Spreadwing	Stokes
Enallagma cyathigerum	Northern Bluet	Stokes
Enallagma civile	Familiar Bluet	Stokes
Enallagma erbium	Marsh Bluet	Stokes
Coenagrion resolutum	Taiga Bluet	Stokes
Ischnura verticalis	Eastern Forktail	Stokes
Ischnura perparva	Western Forktail	Stokes
Ischnura posita	Fragile Forktail	Stokes
Nehalennia Irene	Sedge Sprite	Stokes
Anax junius	Common Green Darner	Dunkle

Butterfly and Moth Species List, Rice Lake NWR (Continued)

Species		
Scientific Name	**Common Name**	**Source**
Boyeria vinosa	Fawn Darner	Dunkle
Aeshna Canadensis	Canada Darner	Dunkle
Aeshna umbrosa	Shadow Darner	Dunkle
Aeshna interrupta	Variable Darner	Dunkle
Basiaeschna janata	Springtime Darner	Dunkle
Ophiogomphus morrisoni	Great Basin Snaketail	Dunkle
Ophiogomphus anomalus	Extra-Striped Snaketail	Dunkle
Ophiogomphus susbehcha	Wisconsin Snaketail	Dunkle
Ophiogomphus carolus	Riffle Snaketail	Dunkle
Ophiogomphus colubrinis	Boreal Snaketail	Dunkle
Ophiogomphus rupinsulensis	Rusty Snaketail	Dunkle
Cordulia shurtleffii	American Emerald	Dunkle
Pantala flavescens	Wandering Glider	Dunkle
Pantala hymenaea	Spot-winged Glider	Dunkle
Libellula lydia	Common Whitetail	Dunkle
Libellula luctuosa	Widow Skimmer	Dunkle
Libellula pulchella	Twelve-spotted Skimmer	*Dunkle*
Libellula quadrimaculata	Four-spotted Skimmer	*Dunkle*
Libellula julia	Chalk-fronted Corporal	*Dunkle*
Erythemis simplicicollis	Eastern Pondhawk	*Dunkle*
Pachydiplax longipennis	Blue Dasher	*Dunkle*
Sympetrum rubicundulum	Ruby Meadowhawk	*Dunkle*
Sympetrum internum	Cherry-Faced Meadowhawk	*Dunkle*
Sympetrum semicinctum	Band-Winged Meadowhawk	*Dunkle*
Sympetrum vicinum	Yellow-Legged Meadowhawk	*Dunkle*
Sympetrum obtrusum	White-faced Meadowhawk	*Dunkle*
Sumpetrum costiferum	Saffron-winged Meadowhawk	*Dunkle*
Sympetrum corruptum	Variegated Meadowhawk	*Dunkle*
Sympetrum danae	Black Meadowhawk	*Dunkle*
Leucorrhinia intacta	Dot-tailed Whiteface	*Dunkle*
Leucorrhinia frigida	Frosted Whiteface	*Dunkle*
Leucorrhinia proxima	Red-Waisted Whiteface	*Dunkle*
Leucorrhinia borealis	Boreal Whiteface	*Dunkle*
Leucorrhinia glacialis	Crimson-ringed Whiteface	*Dunkle*
Leucorrhinia hudsonica	Hudsonian Whiteface	*Dunkle*
Source: Dunkle, Sidney W. Dragonflies through Binoculars: A Field Guide to Dragonflies of North America. 2000. Oxford University Press.		

Dragonfly and Damselfly Species List, Rice Lake NWR

Species		Source
Scientific Name	**Common Name**	
Calopteryx maculata	Ebony Jewelwing	Stokes
Celithemis elisa	Calico Pennant	Dunkle
Celithemis eponina	Halloween Pennant	Dunkle
Tramea lacerata	Black Saddlebags	Dunkle
Perithemis tenera	Eastern Amberwing	Dunkle
Neurocordulia yamaskanensis	Stygian Shadowdragon	Dunkle
Somatochlora franklini	Delicate Emerald	Dunkle
Somatochlora kennedyi	Kennedy's Emerald	Dunkle
Somatochlora forcipata	Forcipate Emerald	Dunkle
Somatochlora ensigera	Plains Emerald	Dunkle
Somatochlora walshii	Brush-tipped Emerald	Dunkle
Somatochlora minor	Ocellated Emerald	Dunkle
Somatochlora elongata	Ski-Tailed Emerald	Dunkle
Somatochlora williamsoni	Williamson's Emerald	Dunkle
Epitheca cynosura	Common Baskettail	Dunkle
Epitheca princeps	Prince Baskettail	Dunkle
Williamsonia fletcheri	Ebony Boghaunter	Dunkle
Dorocordulia libera	Racket-Tailed Emerald	Dunkle
Macromia illinoiensis	Illinois River Cruiser	Dunkle
Didymops transversa	Stream Cruiser	Dunkle
Cordulegaster maculata	Twin-Spotted Spiketail	Dunkle
Arigomphus cornutus	Horned Clubtail	Dunkle
Arigomphus furcifer	Lilypad Clubtail	Dunkle
Dromogomphus spinosus	Black-Shouldered Spinyleg	Dunkle
Stylurus notatus	Elusive Clubtail	Dunkle
Stylurus amnicola	Riverine Clubtail	Dunkle
Stylurus spiniceps	Arrow Clubtail	Dunkle
Gomphus externus	Plains Clubtail	Dunkle
Gomphus fraternus	Midland Clubtail	Dunkle
Gomphus lineatifrons	Splendid Clubtail	Dunkle

Dragonfly and Damselfly Species List, Rice Lake NWR (Continued)

Species		Source
Scientific Name	**Common Name**	
Gomphus vastus	Cobra Clubtail	Dunkle
Gomphus ventricosus	Skillet Clubtail	Dunkle
Gomphus viridifrons	Green-Faced Clubtail	Dunkle
Gomphus adelphus	Mustached Clubtail	Dunkle
Gomphus exilis	Lancet Clubtail	Dunkle
Gomphus Spicatus	Dusky Clubtail	Dunkle
Gomphus lividus	Ashy Clubtail	Dunkle
Gomphus quadricolor	Rapids Clubtail	Dunkle
Gomphus graslinellus	Pronghorn Clubtail	Dunkle
Oplonaeschna armata	Riffle Darner	Dunkle
Aeshna sitchensis	Zigzag Darner	Dunkle
Aeshna verticalis	Green-Striped Darner	Dunkle
Aeshna tuberculifera	Black-Tipped Darner	Dunkle
Aeshna eremita	Lake Darner	Dunkle
Aeshna constricta	Lance-Tipped Darner	Dunkle
Boyeria grafiana	Ocellated Darner	Dunkle
Calopteryx aequabilis	River Jewelwing	Stokes
Lestes disjunctus	Common Spreadwing	Stokes
Lestes congener	Spotted Spreadwing	Stokes
Lestes dryas	Emerald Spreadwing	Stokes
Lestes rectangularis	Slender Spreadwing	Stokes
Enallagma cyathigerum	Northern Bluet	Stokes
Enallagma civile	Familiar Bluet	Stokes
Enallagma erbium	Marsh Bluet	Stokes
Coenagrion resolutum	Taiga Bluet	Stokes
Ischnura verticalis	Eastern Forktail	Stokes
Ischnura perparva	Western Forktail	Stokes
Ischnura posita	Fragile Forktail	Stokes
Nehalennia Irene	Sedge Sprite	Stokes
Anax junius	Common Green Darner	Dunkle

Dragonfly and Damselfly Species List, Rice Lake NWR (Continued)

Species		
Scientific Name	**Common Name**	**Source**
Boyeria vinosa	Fawn Darner	Dunkle
Aeshna Canadensis	Canada Darner	Dunkle
Aeshna umbrosa	Shadow Darner	Dunkle
Aeshna interrupta	Variable Darner	Dunkle
Basiaeschna janata	Springtime Darner	Dunkle
Ophiogomphus morrisoni	Great Basin Snaketail	Dunkle
Ophiogomphus anomalus	Extra-Striped Snaketail	Dunkle
Ophiogomphus susbehcha	Wisconsin Snaketail	Dunkle
Ophiogomphus carolus	Riffle Snaketail	Dunkle
Ophiogomphus colubrinis	Boreal Snaketail	Dunkle
Ophiogomphus rupinsulensis	Rusty Snaketail	Dunkle
Cordulia shurtleffii	American Emerald	Dunkle
Pantala flavescens	Wandering Glider	Dunkle
Pantala hymenaea	Spot-winged Glider	Dunkle
Libellula lydia	Common Whitetail	Dunkle
Libellula luctuosa	Widow Skimmer	Dunkle
Libellula pulchella	Twelve-spotted Skimmer	Dunkle
Libellula quadrimaculata	Four-spotted Skimmer	Dunkle
Libellula julia	Chalk-fronted Corporal	Dunkle
Erythemis simplicicollis	Eastern Pondhawk	Dunkle
Pachydiplax longipennis	Blue Dasher	Dunkle
Sympetrum rubicundulum	Ruby Meadowhawk	Dunkle
Sympetrum internum	Cherry-Faced Meadowhawk	Dunkle
Sympetrum semicinctum	Band-Winged Meadowhawk	Dunkle
Sympetrum vicinum	Yellow-Legged Meadowhawk	Dunkle
Sympetrum obtrusum	White-faced Meadowhawk	Dunkle
Sumpetrum costiferum	Saffron-winged Meadowhawk	Dunkle
Sympetrum corruptum	Variegated Meadowhawk	Dunkle
Sympetrum danae	Black Meadowhawk	Dunkle
Leucorrhinia intacta	Dot-tailed Whiteface	Dunkle

Dragonfly and Damselfly Species List, Rice Lake NWR (Continued)

Species		Source
Scientific Name	**Common Name**	
Leucorrhinia frigida	Frosted Whiteface	Dunkle
Leucorrhinia proxima	Red-Waisted Whiteface	Dunkle
Leucorrhinia borealis	Boreal Whiteface	Dunkle
Leucorrhinia glacialis	Crimson-ringed Whiteface	Dunkle
Leucorrhinia hudsonica	Hudsonian Whiteface	Dunkle
Source: Dunkle, Sidney W. Dragonflies through Binoculars: A Field Guide to Dragonflies of North America. 2000. Oxford University Press.		

Amphibian and Reptile Species List, Rice Lake NWR

Species		Source	Confirmed	Date	Confirmed by
Scientific Name	**Common Name**				
Ambystoma laterale	Blue-spotted salamander	Oldfield 1994			
Ambystoma tigrinum	Tiger salamander	Oldfield 1994			
Plethondon cinereus	Redback salamander	Oldfield 1994			
Bufo americanus	American toad	Oldfield 1994	*	Jun-98	W. Brininger
Hyla chrysoscelis	Cope's gray treefrog		*	May-96	T. Topitchofer
Hyla versicolor	Gray treefrog	Oldfield 1994	*	Apr-01	W. Brininger
Pseudacris crucifer	Spring peeper	Oldfield 1994	*	Apr-01	W. Brininger
Psudacris triseriata	Western chorus frog	Oldfield 1994	*	Apr-01	W. Brininger
Rana clamitans	Green frog	Oldfield 1994			
Rana pipens	Northern leopard frog	Oldfield 1994	*	Apr-01	W. Brininger
Rana septentrionalis	Mink frog	Oldfield 1994	*	Jul-96	T. Topitchofer
Rana sylvatica	Wood frog	Oldfield 1994	*	Apr-01	W. Brininger
Chelydra serpentina	Snapping turtle	Oldfield 1994	*	Aug-02	M. McDowell
Chrysemys picta	Painted turtle	Oldfield 1994	*	Aug-02	M. McDowell
Storeria occipitomaculata	Redbelly snake	Oldfield 1994			
Thamnophis sirtalis	Common garter snake	Oldfield 1994	*	Aug-02	M. McDowell
Oldfield B. and J. Moriarty. 1994. Amphibians and reptiles native to Minnesota. University of Minnesota Press. 237pp.					

Fish Species List, Rice Lake NWR and the Sandstone Unit of Rice Lake NWR

Species		Source	Confirmed	Date	Confirmed by	RCP
Scientific Name	**Common Name**					
Acipenser fulvescens	Lake sturgeon	Phillips, 1982				*
Ictiobus cyprinellus	Bigmouth buffalo	Phillips, 1982	*	80's and 90's	Ashland FRO	
Ictalurus melas	Black bullhead	Phillips, 1982	*	80's and 90's	Ashland FRO	
Pomoxis nigromaculatus	Black crappie	Phillips, 1982	*	80's and 90's	Ashland FRO	
Lepomis gibbosus	Pumpkinseed	Phillips, 1982	*	Dec-05	MNDNR Fisheries	
Lepomis macrochirus	Bluegill	Phillips, 1982	*	80's and 90's	Ashland FRO	
Ictalurus nebulosus	Brown bullhead	Phillips, 1982	*	80's and 90's	Ashland FRO	
Culaea inconstans	Brook stickleback	Phillips, 1982	*	80's and 90's	Ashland FRO	
Salvelinus fontinalis	Brook trout	Phillips, 1982				*
Amia calva	Bowfin	Phillips, 1982	*	80's and 90's	Ashland FRO	
Lota lota	Burbot	Phillips, 1982	*	80's and 90's	Ashland FRO	
Urbra limi	Central mudminnow	Phillips, 1982	*	80's and 90's	Ashland FRO	
Notropis cornutus	Common shiner	Phillips, 1982	*	80's and 90's	Ashland FRO	
Pimephales promelas	Fathead minnow	Phillips, 1982	*	80's and 90's	Ashland FRO	
Notemigonus crysoleucas	Golden shiner	Phillips, 1982	*	80's and 90's	Ashland FRO	
Micropterus salmoides	Largemouth bass	Phillips, 1982	*	80's and 90's	Ashland FRO	
Esox lucius	Northern pike	Phillips, 1982	*	80's and 90's	Ashland FRO	
Notropis unbratilis	Redfin shiner	Phillips, 1982	*	80's and 90's	Ashland FRO	
Ambloplites rupestris	Rock bass	Phillips, 1982	*	80's and 90's	Ashland FRO	
Noturus gyrinus	Tadpole madtom	Phillips, 1982	*	80's and 90's	Ashland FRO	
Stizostedion vitreum	Walleye	Phillips, 1982	*	80's and 90's	Ashland FRO	
Catosomus commersoni	White sucker	Phillips, 1982	*	80's and 90's	Ashland FRO	
Perca flavescens	Yellow perch	Phillips, 1982	*	80's and 90's	Ashland FRO	
Phillips, Gary L. 1982. Fishes of the Minnesota region. Universily of Minnesota Press. Minneapolis, Minnesota. 248 pp.						

Mollusk and Crustacean Species List, Rice Lake NWR and the Sandstone Unit of Rice Lake NWR

Species						
Scientific Name	Common Name	Source	Confirmed	Date	Confirmed by	RCP
Alasmidonta marginata	Elktoe	Sietman 2003				*
Amblema plicata	Threeridge	Sietman 2003				*
Fusconia flava	Wabash pigtoe	Cummings 1992				
Pyganodon grandis	Giant floater	Cummings 1992, Sietman 2003	*	7/8/04	R3 FRO*	
Anodontoides ferussacianus	Cylindrical papershell	Cummings 1992, Sietman 2003				
Strophitus undulatus	Strange floater	Cummings 1992, Sietman 2003	*	7/8/04	R3 FRO	
Lasmigona complanata	White heelsplitter	Cummings 1992, Sietman 2003				
Lasmigona costata	Fluted-shell	Cummings 1992				
Lasmigona compressa	Creek heelsplitter	Cummings 1992, Sietman 2003				
Actinonaias ligamentina	Mucket	Cummings 1992				
Ligumia recta	Black sandshell	Cummings 1992, Sietman 2003				*
Pleurobema coccineum	Round pigtoe	Sietman 2003				*
Lampsilis siliquoidea	Fatmucket	Cummings 1992, Sietman 2003	*	7/8/04	R3 FRO	
Lampsilis cardium	Plain pocketbook	Cummings 1992, Sietman 2003				
Utterbackia imbecillis	Paper pondshell		*	7/8/04	R3 FRO	
Sphaeridae sp.	Fingernail clams		*	7/8/04	R3 FRO	
	Possible new species, still being checked		*	7/8/04	R3 FRO	
Dresissena polymorpha	Zebra mussel					*
Vertigo bollesiana	Snail (no common name)					*
Vertigo cristata	Snail (no common name)					*
Vertigo morsei	Snail (no common name)					*
Vertigo paradoxa	Snail (no common name)					*
Orconectes rusticus	Rusty crayfish					*
Literature Cited Sietman, B. 2003. Field guide to the freshwater mussels of Minnesota. State of Minnesota, Department of Natural Resources. 144pp. Cummings, K. and C. Mayer. 1992. Field guide to freshwater mussels of the Midwest. Illinois Natural History Survey Manual 5. 194pp. *Region 3 Fisheries Resources Office staff were Scott Yess (LaCrosse) and Glenn Miller (Ashland)						

Bird Species List, Rice Lake NWR

Species Scientific Name	Common Name	Source	Confirmed	Date	Confirmed By	RCP
Gavia immer	Common Loon	Sibley, 2000	*	4/11/94	C. Lapp	*
Podiceps grisegena	Red-necked Grebe	Sibley, 2000	*	4/24/96	C. Lapp	
Podiceps auritus	Horned Grebe	Sibley, 2000	*	10/10/02	W. Nelson	
Podiceps nigricollis	Eared Grebe	Sibley, 2000	*	4/24/96	C. Lapp	
Podilymbus podiceps	Pied-billed Grebe	Sibley, 2000	*	4/11/94	C. Lapp	
Pelecanus erythrorhynchos	American White Pelican	Sibley, 2000	*	4/21/94	C. Lapp	
Phalacrocorax auritus	Double-crested Cormorant	Sibley, 2000	*	4/29/94	C. Lapp	*
Botaurus lentiginosus	American Bittern	Sibley, 2000	*	5/5/94	C. Lapp	*
Ixobrychus exilis	Least Bittern	Sibley, 2000	*	Jun-01	MCBS	*
Ardea herodias	Great Blue Heron	Sibley, 2000	*	4/11/94	C. Lapp	
Ardea alba	Great Egret	Sibley, 2000	*	4/24/96	C. Lapp	
Bubulcus ibis	Cattle Egret		*	8/7/06	D. Huhta	
Butorides virescens	Green Heron	Sibley, 2000	*	5/18/94	C. Lapp	
Nycticorax nycticorax	Black-crowned Night-Heron	Sibley, 2000				*
Cygnus buccinator	Trumpeter Swan	Sibley, 2000	*	4/11/94	C. Lapp	*
Cygnus columbianus	Tundra Swan	Sibley, 2000	*	3/30/99	W. Brininger	
Branta canadensis	Canada Goose	Sibley, 2000	*	4/11/94	C. Lapp	*
Anser albifrons	Greater White-fronted Goose	Sibley, 2000	*	9/16/02	M. McDowell	
Chen rossii	Ross's Goose		*	1996	Refuge staff	
Chen caerulescens	Snow Goose	Sibley, 2000	*	9/25/96	C. Lapp	*
Aix sponsa	Wood Duck	Sibley, 2000	*	4/11/94	C. Lapp	*
Anas platyrhynchos	Mallard	Sibley, 2000	*	4/11/94	C. Lapp	*
Anas rubripes	American Black Duck	Sibley, 2000	*	4/24/96	C. Lapp	
Anas strepera	Gadwall	Sibley, 2000	*	4/24/96	C. Lapp	
Anas acuta	Northern Pintail	Sibley, 2000	*	4/25/96	C. Lapp	*
Anas americana	American Wigeon	Sibley, 2000	*	4/21/94	C. Lapp	
Anas clypeata	Northern Shoveler	Sibley, 2000	*	4/21/94	C. Lapp	

Bird Species List, Rice Lake NWR (Continued)

Species Scientific Name	Common Name	Source	Confirmed	Date	Confirmed By	RCP
Anas discors	Blue-winged Teal	Sibley, 2000	*	4/21/94	C. Lapp	*
Anas crecca	Green-winged Teal	Sibley, 2000	*	4/11/94	C. Lapp	
Aythya valisineria	Canvasback	Sibley, 2000	*	4/29/94	C. Lapp	*
Aythya americana	Redhead	Sibley, 2000	*	4/21/94	C. Lapp	
Aythya collaris	Ring-necked Duck	Sibley, 2000	*	4/11/94	C. Lapp	
Aythya marila	Greater Scaup	Sibley, 2000	*	5/15/87	W. Nelson	
Aythya affinis	Lesser Scaup	Sibley, 2000	*	4/21/94	C. Lapp	*
Bucephala clangula	Common Goldeneye	Sibley, 2000	*	4/11/94	C. Lapp	
Bucphala albeola	Bufflehead	Sibley, 2000	*	4/11/94	C. Lapp	
Lophodytes cucullatus	Hooded Merganser	Sibley, 2000	*	4/11/94	C. Lapp	
Mergus merganser	Common Merganser	Sibley, 2000	*	4/11/94	C. Lapp	
Mergus serrator	Red-breasted Merganser	Sibley, 2000				
Melanitta fusca	White-winged Scoter		*	1941	Refuge staff	
Oxyura jamaicensis	Ruddy Duck	Sibley, 2000	*	9/13/84	W. Nelson	
Cathartes aura	Turkey Vulture	Sibley, 2000	*	4/21/94	C. Lapp	
Circus cyaneus	Northern Harrier	Sibley, 2000	*	4/11/94	C. Lapp	*
Accipiter striatus	Sharp-shinned Hawk	Sibley, 2000	*	5/5/94	C. Lapp	
Accipiter cooperii	Cooper's Hawk	Sibley, 2000	*	5/5/94	C. Lapp	
Accipiter gentilis	Northern Goshawk	Sibley, 2000	*	9/25/01	W. Brininger	*
Buteo lineatus	Red-shouldered Hawk	Sibley, 2000	*	Jun-01	MCBS	*
Buteo platypterus	Broad-winged Hawk	Sibley, 2000	*	Jun-92	NRRI	
Buteo jamaicensis	Red-tailed Hawk	Sibley, 2000	*	4/11/94	C. Lapp	
Buteo regalis	Ferruginous Hawk		*	8/29/89	Visitor	
Buteo lagopus	Rough-legged Hawk	Sibley, 2000	*	1/4/03	M. McDowell	
Aquila chrysaetos	Golden Eagle	Sibley, 2000	*	4/11/94	C. Lapp	
Haliaeetus leucocephalus	Bald Eagle	Sibley, 2000	*	4/11/94	C. Lapp	*
Pandion haliaetus	Osprey	Sibley, 2000	*	4/21/94	C. Lapp	
Falco columbarius	Merlin	Sibley, 2000	*	9/28/98	W. Brininger	
Falco sparverius	American Kestrel	Sibley, 2000	*	4/11/94	C. Lapp	

Bird Species List, Rice Lake NWR (Continued)

Species Scientific Name	Common Name	Source	Confirmed	Date	Confirmed By	RCP
Falco peregrinus	Peregrine Falcon	Sibley, 2000	*	5/17/95	C. Lapp	*
Phasianus colchicus	Ring-necked Pheasant	Sibley, 2000	*	1941	Refuge staff	
Tympanuchus phasianellus	Sharp-tailed Grouse	Sibley, 2000	*	4/21/94	C. Lapp	
Tympanuchus cupido	Greater Prairie-Chicken		*	1941	Refuge staff	
Bonasa umbellus	Ruffed Grouse	Sibley, 2000	*	Jun-92	NRRI	
Falcipennis canadensis	Spruce Grouse		*	7/2/03	Yves Cormier	
Fulica americana	American Coot	Sibley, 2000	*	Jun-92	NRRI	
Rallus limicola	Virginia Rail	Sibley, 2000	*	5/30/94	C. Lapp	
Porzana carolina	Sora	Sibley, 2000	*	Jun-92	NRRI	
Coturnicops noveboracensis	Yellow Rail	Sibley, 2000	*	5/18/94	C. Lapp	*
Grus americana	Whooping Crane		*	1981	W. Nelson	
Grus canadensis	Sandhill Crane (Greater)	Sibley, 2000	*	4/11/94	C. Lapp	
Pluvialis squatarola	Black-bellied Plover	Sibley, 2000	*	5/25/94	C. Lapp	
Pluvialis dominica	American Golden-Plover	Sibley, 2000	*	1941	Refuge staff	
Charadrius semipalmatus	Semipalmated Plover	Sibley, 2000	*	8/29/95	C. Lapp	
Charadrius vociferus	Killdeer	Sibley, 2000	*	4/11/94	C. Lapp	
Tringa melanoleuca	Greater Yellowlegs	Sibley, 2000	*	5/5/94	C. Lapp	*
Tringa flavipes	Lesser Yellowlegs	Sibley, 2000	*	5/5/94	C. Lapp	
Tringa solitaria	Solitary Sandpiper	Sibley, 2000	*	5/5/94	C. Lapp	
Actitis macularia	Spotted Sandpiper	Sibley, 2000	*	5/18/94	C. Lapp	
Limosa haemastica	Hudsonian Godwit	Janssen, 1987				*
Limosa fedoa	Marbled Godwit	Sibley, 2000	*	5/30/03	M. McDowell	*
Bartramia longicauda	Upland Sandpiper	Sibley, 2000	*	1941	Refuge staff	*
Numenius phaeopus	Whimbrel	Janssen, 1987				*
Arenaria interpres	Ruddy Turnstone	Sibley, 2000	*	5/18/94	C. Lapp	
Calidris alba	Sanderling	Sibley, 2000				
Calidris alpina	Dunlin	Sibley, 2000	*	5/17/95	C. Lapp	
Calidris melanotos	Pectoral Sandpiper	Sibley, 2000	*	9/12/96	C. Lapp	
Calidris fuscicollis	White-rumped Sandpiper	Sibley, 2000				

Bird Species List, Rice Lake NWR (Continued)

Species Scientific Name	Common Name	Source	Confirmed	Date	Confirmed By	RCP
Calidris pusilla	Semipalmated Sandpiper	Sibley, 2000	*	5/18/94	C. Lapp	
Calidris minutilla	Least Sandpiper	Sibley, 2000	*	6/8/94	C. Lapp	
Calidris himantopus	Stilt Sandpiper	Sibley, 2000	*	5/17/95	C. Lapp	*
Limnodromus scolopaceus	Long-billed Dowitcher	Sibley, 2000				
Limnodromus griseus	Short-billed Dowitcher	Sibley, 2000	*	5/15/04	W. Nelson	*
Tryngites subruficollis	Buff-breasted Sandpiper	Janssen, 1987	*	8/17/06	Jacob Randa	*
Scolopax minor	American Woodcock	Sibley, 2000	*	5/8/80	K. Burns	*
Gallinago gallinago	Common Snipe	Sibley, 2000	*	5/20/02	M. Stefanski	
Phalaropus tricolor	Wilson's Phalarope	Sibley, 2000				*
Phalaropus lobatus	Red-necked Phalarope	Sibley, 2000				
Larus philadephia	Bonaparte's Gull	Sibley, 2000	*	5/5/94	C. Lapp	
Larus pipixcan	Franklin's Gull	Sibley, 2000				
Larus delawarensis	Ring-billed Gull	Sibley, 2000	*	4/11/94	C. Lapp	*
Larus argentatus	Herring Gull	Sibley, 2000	*	9/23/03	M. McDowell	
Sterna caspia	Caspian Tern	Sibley, 2000	*	5/10/03	M. McDowell	
Sterna hirundo	Common Tern	Sibley, 2000	*	5/25/94	C. Lapp	*
Sterna forsteri	Forster's Tern	Sibley, 2000				*
Chlidonias niger	Black Tern	Sibley, 2000	*	Jul-93	C. Lapp	*
Zenaida macroura	Mourning Dove	Sibley, 2000	*	Jun-01	MCBS	
Coccyzus americanus	Yellow-billed Cuckoo	Sibley, 2000				
Coccyzus erythropthalmus	Black-billed Cuckoo	Sibley, 2000	*	Jun-92	NRRI	*
Asio otus	Long-eared Owl	Sibley, 2000				*
Asio flammeus	Short-eared Owl	Sibley, 2000	*	4/27/99	W. Brininger	*
Bubo virginianus	Great-horned Owl	Sibley, 2000	*	4/11/94	C. Lapp	
Nyctea scandiaca	Snowy Owl	Sibley, 2000	*	11/20/01	W. Brininger	
Strix nebulosa	Great Gray Owl	Sibley, 2000	*	12/8/04	M. McDowell	
Strix varia	Barred Owl	Sibley, 2000	*	5/10/03	J. Blanich	
Aegolius funereus	Boreal Owl	Sibley, 2000				
Aegolius acadicus	Northern Saw-whet Owl	Sibley, 2000	*	3/15/03	M. McDowell	

Bird Species List, Rice Lake NWR (Continued)

Species Scientific Name	Common Name	Source	Confirmed	Date	Confirmed By	RCP
Otus asio	Eastern Screech-Owl	Sibley, 2000	*	7/14/02	J. & B. Neal	
Sturnia ulula	Northern Hawk Owl	Sibley, 2000	*	11/2/04	D. Huhta	
Caprimulgus vociferus	Whip-poor-will	Sibley, 2000	*	1941	Refuge staff	*
Chordeiles minor	Common Nighthawk	Sibley, 2000	*	Jun-03	M. McDowell	
Chaetura pelagica	Chimney Swift	Sibley, 2000	*	Jun-01	MCBS	
Archilochus colubris	Ruby-throated Hummingbird	Sibley, 2000	*	Jun-96	J. Brink	
Ceryle alcyon	Belted Kingfisher	Sibley, 2000	*	5/10/03	M. McDowell	
Melanerpes erythrocephalus	Red-headed Woodpecker	Sibley, 2000	*	6/17/84	W. Nelson	*
Melanerpes carolinus	Red-bellied Woodpecker	Sibley, 2000	*	6/5/01	J. Brink	
Sphyrapicus varius	Yellow-bellied Sapsucker	Sibley, 2000	*	Jun-92	NRRI	
Picoides pubescens	Downy Woodpecker	Sibley, 2000	*	Jun-92	NRRI	
Picoides villosus	Hairy Woodpecker	Sibley, 2000	*	Jun-92	NRRI	
Picoides arcticus	Black-backed Woodpecker	Sibley, 2000				
Colaptes auratus	Northern Flicker	Sibley, 2000	*	Jun-92	NRRI	*
Dryocopus pileatus	Pileated Woodpecker	Sibley, 2000	*	Jun-92	NRRI	
Contopus cooperi	Olive-sided Flycatcher	Sibley, 2000	*	5/26/87	W. Nelson	*
Contopus virens	Eastern Wood-Pewee	Sibley, 2000	*	Jun-92	NRRI	
Empidonax flaviventris	Yellow-bellied Flycatcher	Sibley, 2000	*	5/26/87	W. Nelson	
Empidonax alnorum	Alder Flycatcher	Sibley, 2000	*	Jun-92	NRRI	
Empidonax minimus	Least Flycatcher	Sibley, 2000	*	Jun-92	NRRI	
Sayornis phoebe	Eastern Phoebe	Sibley, 2000	*	Jun-92	NRRI	
Sayornis saya	Say's Phoebe		*	Oct-05	M. McDowell	
Myiarchus crinitus	Great Crested Flycatcher	Sibley, 2000	*	Jun-92	NRRI	
Tyrannus tyrannus	Eastern Kingbird	Sibley, 2000	*	Jun-01	MCBS	
Tyrannus verticalis	Western Kingbird	Sibley, 2000				
Lanius excubitor	Northern Shrike	Sibley, 2000	*	1/4/03	M. McDowell	
Vireo olivaceus	Red-eyed Vireo	Sibley, 2000	*	Jun-92	NRRI	
Vireo gilvus	Warbling Vireo	Sibley, 2000	*	Jun-01	MCBS	
Vireo philadelphicus	Philadelphia Vireo	Sibley, 2000	*	5/20/95	MOU group	

Bird Species List, Rice Lake NWR (Continued)

Species Scientific Name	Common Name	Source	Confirmed	Date	Confirmed By	RCP
Vireo flavifrons	Yellow-throated Vireo	Sibley, 2000	*	Jun-92	NRRI	
Vireo solitarius	Blue-headed Vireo	Sibley, 2000	*	5/28/91	W. Nelson	
Cyanocitta cristata	Blue Jay	Sibley, 2000	*	Jun-92	NRRI	
Perisoreus canadensis	Gray Jay	Sibley, 2000	*	10/1/86	J. Francis	
Pica hudsonia	Black-billed Magpie	Sibley, 2000	*	1/26/87	D. Heffernan	
Corvus corax	Common Raven	Sibley, 2000	*	Jun-96	J. Brink	
Corvus brachyrhynchos	American Crow	Sibley, 2000	*	Jun-92	NRRI	
Eremophila alpestris	Horned Lark	Sibley, 2000	*	10/19/03	M. McDowell	
Progne subis	Purple Martin	Sibley, 2000	*	5/23/98	J. Blanich	
Stelgiopteryx serripennis	Northern Rough-winged Swallow	Sibley, 2000	*	5/17/02	Aitkin Ornithology Class	
Riparia riparia	Bank Swallow	Sibley, 2000	*	1941	Refuge staff	
Tachycineta bicolor	Tree Swallow	Sibley, 2000	*	5/10/03	M. McDowell	
Petrochelidon pyrrhonota	Cliff Swallow	Sibley, 2000	*	5/10/03	M. McDowell	
Hirundo rustica	Barn Swallow	Sibley, 2000	*	5/10/03	M. McDowell	
Poecile atricapilla	Black-capped Chickadee	Sibley, 2000	*	Jun-92	NRRI	
Poecile hudsonica	Boreal Chickadee	Sibley, 2000				
Sitta canadensis	Red-breasted Nuthatch	Sibley, 2000	*	Jun-92	NRRI	
Sitta carolinensis	White-breasted Nuthatch	Sibley, 2000	*	Jun-92	NRRI	
Certhia americana	Brown Creeper	Sibley, 2000	*	Jun-92	NRRI	
Troglodytes aedon	House Wren	Sibley, 2000	*	Jun-01	MCBS	
Troglodytes troglodytes	Winter Wren	Sibley, 2000	*	Jun-92	NRRI	
Cistrothorus platensis	Sedge Wren	Sibley, 2000	*	Jun-92	NRRI	*
Cistothorus palustris	Marsh Wren	Sibley, 2000	*	Jun-01	MCBS	
Regulus satrapa	Golden-crowned Kinglet	Sibley, 2000	*	Jun-92	NRRI	
Reugus calendula	Ruby-crowned Kinglet	Sibley, 2000	*	4/27/99	W. Brininger	
Polioptila caerulea	Blue-gray Gnatcatcher	Sibley, 2000	*	5/15/04	M. McDowell	

Bird Species List, Rice Lake NWR (Continued)

Species Scientific Name	Common Name	Source	Confirmed	Date	Confirmed By	RCP
Sialia mexicana	Western Bluebird			1950-1955	Conservation Volunteer, March-Apr 1955	
Sialia sialis	Eastern Bluebird	Sibley, 2000	*	Jun-01	MCBS	
Turdus migratorius	American Robin	Sibley, 2000	*	Jun-92	NRRI	
Hylocichla mustelina	Wood Thrush	Sibley, 2000	*	Jun-92	NRRI	*
Catharus fuscescens	Veery	Sibley, 2000	*	Jun-92	NRRI	
Catharus ustulatus	Swainson's Thrush	Sibley, 2000	*	5/20/95	MOU group	
Catharus minimus	Gray-cheeked Thrush	Sibley, 2000	*	5/15/04	P. Perry	
Catharus guttatus	Hermit Thrush	Sibley, 2000	*	Jun-92	NRRI	
Dumetella carolinensis	Gray Catbird	Sibley, 2000	*	Jun-92	NRRI	
Mimus polyglottos	Northern Mockingbird		*	5/14/03	M. McDowell	
Toxostoma rufum	Brown Thrasher	Sibley, 2000	*	9/15/03	M. McDowell	
Sturnus vulgaris	European Starling	Sibley, 2000	*	5/10/03	J. Blanich	
Anthus rubescens	American Pipit	Sibley, 2000	*	Oct-88	W. Nelson	
Bombycilla garrulus	Bohemian Waxwing	Sibley, 2000	*	3/16/03	M. McDowell	
Bombycilla cedrorum	Cedar Waxwing	Sibley, 2000	*	Jun-92	NRRI	
Parula americana	Northern Parula	Sibley, 2000	*	Jun-92	NRRI	
Vermivora celata	Orange-crowned Warbler	Sibley, 2000	*	5/10/03	J. Blanich	
Vermivora peregrina	Tennessee Warbler	Sibley, 2000	*	Jun-94	W. Nelson	
Vermivora chrysoptera	Golden-winged Warbler	Sibley, 2000	*	Jun-92	NRRI	*
Vermivora pinus x chrysoptera	Blue-winged x Golden-winged Warbler		*	6/1/03	M. McDowell	
Vermivora ruficapilla	Nashville Warbler	Sibley, 2000	*	Jun-92	NRRI	
Dendroica petechia	Yellow Warbler	Sibley, 2000	*	Jun-92	NRRI	
Dendroica pensylvanica	Chestnut-sided Warbler	Sibley, 2000	*	Jun-92	NRRI	
Dendroica magnolia	Magnolia Warbler	Sibley, 2000	*	Jun-92	NRRI	
Dendroica caerulescens	Black-throated Blue Warbler		*	Jun-92	NRRI	
Dendroica tigrina	Cape May Warbler	Sibley, 2000	*	5/11/03	M. McDowell	

Bird Species List, Rice Lake NWR (Continued)

Species Scientific Name	Common Name	Source	Confirmed	Date	Confirmed By	RCP
Dendroica fusca	Blackburnian Warbler	Sibley, 2000	*	Jun-92	NRRI	
Dendroica coronata	Yellow-rumped Warbler	Sibley, 2000	*	Jun-92	NRRI	
Dendroica virens	Black-throated Green Warbler	Sibley, 2000	*	Jun-92	NRRI	
Dendroica palmarum	Palm Warbler	Sibley, 2000	*	Jun-92	NRRI	
Dendroica pinus	Pine Warbler	Sibley, 2000	*	5/23/98	J. Blanich	
Dendroica castanea	Bay-breasted Warbler	Sibley, 2000	*	5/18/94	W. Nelson	
Dendroica striata	Blackpoll Warbler	Sibley, 2000	*	5/22/03	Aitkin Ornithology Class	
Mniotita varia	Balck-and-white Warbler	Sibley, 2000	*	Jun-92	NRRI	
Setophaga ruticilla	American Redstart	Sibley, 2000	*	Jun-92	NRRI	
Seiurus aurocapillus	Ovenbird	Sibley, 2000	*	Jun-92	NRRI	
Seiurus noveboracensis	Northern Waterthrush	Sibley, 2000	*	Jun-92	NRRI	
Oporornis agilis	Connecticut Warbler	Sibley, 2000	*	May-79	W. Nelson	*
Oporornis philadelphia	Mourning Warbler	Sibley, 2000	*	Jun-92	NRRI	
Geothlypis trichas	Common Yellowthroat	Sibley, 2000	*	Jun-92	NRRI	
Wilsonia pusilla	Wilson's Warbler	Sibley, 2000	*	5/17/03	C. Olson, J. Wozniak	
Wilsonia canadensis	Canada Warbler	Sibley, 2000	*	Jun-92	NRRI	*
Piranga olivacea	Scarlet Tanager	Sibley, 2000	*	Jun-92	NRRI	
Spiza americana	Dickcissel		*	6/16/03	N. Fittinghoff	*
Cardinalis cardinalis	Northern Cardinal	Sibley, 2000	*	5/24/84	J. Francis	
Pheucticus ludovicianus	Rose-breasted Grosbeak	Sibley, 2000	*	Jun-92	NRRI	
Passerina cyanea	Indigo Bunting	Sibley, 2000	*	Jun-92	NRRI	
Pipilo erythrophthalmus	Eastern Towhee	Sibley, 2000	*	5/22/03	Aitkin Ornithology Class	
Spizella arborea	American Tree Sparrow	Sibley, 2000	*	9/18/01	J. Brink	
Spizella pusilla	Field Sparrow	Sibley, 2000	*	5/29/06	W. Nelson	*
Spizella pallida	Clay-colored Sparrow	Sibley, 2000	*	5/10/03	M. McDowell	
Spizella passerina	Chipping Sparrow	Sibley, 2000	*	Jun-92	NRRI	

Bird Species List, Rice Lake NWR (Continued)

Species Scientific Name	Common Name	Source	Confirmed	Date	Confirmed By	RCP
Ammodramus savannarum	Grasshopper Sparrow	Sibley, 2000	*	6/26/86	W. Nelson	*
Ammodramus henslowii	Henslow's Sparrow		*	6/27/86	K. Eckert	*
Ammodramus leconteii	Le Conte's Sparrow	Sibley, 2000	*	5/10/03	M. McDowell	*
Ammodramus nelsoni	Nelson's Sharp-tailed Sparrow		*	6/16/04	M. McDowell	*
Passerculus sanwichensis	Savannah Sparrow	Sibley, 2000	*	5/10/03	M. McDowell	
Pooecetes gramineus	Vesper Sparrow	Sibley, 2000	*	6/12/01	W. Nelson	
Chondestes grammacus	Lark Sparrow		*	5/27/04	M. McDowell	
Zonotrichia querula	Harris's Sparrow	Sibley, 2000	*	9/26/03	M. McDowell	
Zonotrichia albicollis	White-throated Sparrow	Sibley, 2000	*	Jun-92	NRRI	
Zonotrichia leucophrys	White-crowned Sparrow	Sibley, 2000	*	5/10/03	M. McDowell	
Passerella iliaca	Fox Sparrow	Sibley, 2000	*	4/19/01	W. Brininger	
Melospiza melodia	Song Sparrow	Sibley, 2000	*	Jun-92	NRRI	
Melospiza lincolnii	Lincoln's Sparrow	Sibley, 2000	*	10/10/00	W. Nelson	
Melospiza georgiana	Swamp Sparrow	Sibley, 2000	*	Jun-92	NRRI	
Junco hyemalis	Dark-eyed Junco	Sibley, 2000	*	10/15/03	M. McDowell	
Calcarius pictus	Smith's Longspur	Sibley, 2000	*	10/12/02	W. Nelson	
Calcarius lapponicus	Lapland Longspur	Sibley, 2000	*	10/8/03	M. McDowell	
Plectrophenax nivalis	Snow Bunting	Sibley, 2000	*	10/15/03	M. McDowell	
Sturnella neglecta	Western Meadowlark	Sibley, 2000				*
Sturnella magna	Eastern Meadowlark	Sibley, 2000	*	6/8/01	J. Brink	*
Dolichonyx oryzivorus	Bobolink	Sibley, 2000	*	5/10/03	M. McDowell	*
Molothrus ater	Brown-headed Cowbird	Sibley, 2000	*	Jun-92	NRRI	
Xanthocephalus xanthocephalus	Yellow-headed Blackbird	Sibley, 2000	*	Jun-01	MCBS	
Agelaius phoeniceus	Red-winged Blackbird	Sibley, 2000	*	Jun-01	MCBS	
Euphagus cyanocephalus	Brewer's Blackbird	Sibley, 2000	*	Jun-01	MCBS	
Euphagus carolinus	Rusty Blackbird	Sibley, 2000	*	9/28/99	W. Nelson	
Quiscalus quiscula	Common Grackle	Sibley, 2000	*	Jun-01	MCBS	
Icterus bullockii	Bullock's Oriole		*	5/22/03	M. Stefanski	
Icterus galbula	Baltimore Oriole	Sibley, 2000	*	Jun-92	NRRI	

Bird Species List, Rice Lake NWR (Continued)

Species Scientific Name	Common Name	Source	Confirmed	Date	Confirmed By	RCP
Icterus spurius	Orchard Oriole	Sibley, 2000				*
Coccothraustes vespertinus	Evening Grosbeak	Sibley, 2000	*	12/5/01	J. Brink	
Pinicola enucleator	Pine Grosbeak	Sibley, 2000	*	12/2/03	M. McDowell	
Carpodacus purpureus	Purple Finch	Sibley, 2000	*	10/10/01	J. Brink	
Carpodacus mexicanus	House Finch	Sibley, 2000	*	9/24/01	J. Brink	
Loxia curvirostra	Red Crossbill	Sibley, 2000	*	Oct-78	W. Nelson	
Loxia leucoptera	White-winged Crossbill	Sibley, 2000				
Carduelis flammea	Common Redpoll	Sibley, 2000	*	11/27/01	J. Brink	
Carduelis hornemanni	Hoary Redpoll	Sibley, 2000	*	12/2/03	M. McDowell	
Carduelis pinus	Pine Siskin	Sibley, 2000	*	Jun-01	MCBS	
Caruelis tristis	American Goldfinch	Sibley, 2000	*	Jan-03	M. McDowell	
Passer domesticus	House Sparrow	Sibley, 2000	*	Jan-03	J. Brink	

Literature Cited

Sibley, D. 2000. National Audubon Society The Sibley Guide to Birds. Alfred A. Knopf, Inc. New York. 544 pp.

Janssen, R. 1987. Birds in Minnesota. University of Minnesota. Minneapolis, Minnesota. 352 pp.

NRRI = Natural Resources Reseach Institute, University of Minnesota, Duluth

MCBS = Minnesota County Biological Survey, Minnesota Department of Natural Resources

MOU = Minnesota Ornithological Union

Sandstone Unit of Rice Lake NWR Bird Species List

Species						
Scientific Name	Common Name	Source	Confirmed	Date	Confirmed by	RCP
Gavia immer	Common Loon	Sibley, 2000				*
Podiceps grisegena	Red-necked Grebe	Sibley, 2000				
Podiceps auritus	Horned Grebe	Sibley, 2000				
Podiceps nigricollis	Eared Grebe	Sibley, 2000				
Podilymbus podiceps	Pied-billed Grebe	Sibley, 2000				
Pelecanus erythrorhynchos	American White Pelican	Sibley, 2000				
Phalacrocorax auritus	Double-crested Cormorant	Sibley, 2000				*
Botaurus lentiginosus	American Bittern	Sibley, 2000				*
Ixobrychus exilis	Least Bittern	Sibley, 2000				*
Ardea herodias	Great Blue Heron	Sibley, 2000				
Ardea alba	Great Egret	Sibley, 2000				
Butorides virescens	Green Heron	Sibley, 2000				
Nycticorax nycticorax	Black-crowned Night-Heron	Sibley, 2000				*
Cygnus buccinator	Trumpeter Swan	Sibley, 2000	*	3/25/04	M. McDowell	*
Cygnus columbianus	Tundra Swan	Sibley, 2000				
Branta canadensis	Canada Goose	Sibley, 2000	*	3/25/04	M. McDowell	*
Anser albifrons	Greater White-fronted Goose	Sibley, 2000				
Chen caerulescens	Snow Goose	Sibley, 2000				*
Aix sponsa	Wood Duck	Sibley, 2000	*	Jul-92	NRRI	*
Anas platyrhynchos	Mallard	Sibley, 2000				*
Anas rubripes	American Black Duck	Sibley, 2000				
Anas strepera	Gadwall	Sibley, 2000				
Anas acuta	Northern Pintail	Sibley, 2000				*
Anas americana	American Wigeon	Sibley, 2000				
Anas clypeata	Northern Shoveler	Sibley, 2000				
Anas discors	Blue-winged Teal	Sibley, 2000	*	May-92	NRRI	*
Anas crecca	Green-winged Teal	Sibley, 2000				
Aythya valisineria	Canvasback	Sibley, 2000				*
Aythya americana	Redhead	Sibley, 2000				

Sandstone Unit of Rice Lake NWR Bird Species List (Continued)

Species					
Scientific Name	Common Name	Source	Confirmed	Date	Confirmed by	RCP
Aythya collaris	Ring-necked Duck	Sibley, 2000				
Aythya marila	Greater Scaup	Sibley, 2000				
Aythya affinis	Lesser Scaup	Sibley, 2000				*
Bucephala clangula	Common Goldeneye	Sibley, 2000				
Bucephala albeola	Bufflehead	Sibley, 2000				
Lophodytes cucullatus	Hooded Merganser	Sibley, 2000				
Mergus merganser	Common Merganser	Sibley, 2000				
Mergus serrator	Red-breasted Merganser	Sibley, 2000				
Oxyura jamaicensis	Ruddy Duck	Sibley, 2000				
Cathartes aura	Turkey Vulture	Sibley, 2000				
Circus cyaneus	Northern Harrier	Sibley, 2000	*	May-92	NRRI	*
Accipiter striatus	Sharp-shinned Hawk	Sibley, 2000				
Accipiter cooperii	Cooper's Hawk	Sibley, 2000				
Accipiter gentilis	Northern Goshawk	Sibley, 2000				*
Buteo lineatus	Red-shouldered Hawk	Sibley, 2000				*
Buteo platypterus	Broad-winged Hawk	Sibley, 2000	*	Jun-92	NRRI	
Buteo jamaicensis	Red-tailed Hawk	Sibley, 2000	*	Jul-92	NRRI	
Buteo lagopus	Rough-legged Hawk	Sibley, 2000				
Aquila chrysaetos	Golden Eagle	Sibley, 2000				
Haliaeetus leucocephalus	Bald Eagle	Sibley, 2000	*	3/25/04	M. McDowell	*
Pandion haliaetus	Osprey	Sibley, 2000				
Falco columbarius	Merlin	Sibley, 2000				
Falco sparverius	American Kestrel	Sibley, 2000				
Falco peregrinus	Peregrine Falcon	Sibley, 2000				*
Meleagris gallopavo	Wild Turkey	Sibley, 2000	*	3/25/04	M. McDowell	
Phasianus colchicus	Ring-necked Pheasant	Sibley, 2000				
Tympanuchus phasianellus	Sharp-tailed Grouse	Sibley, 2000	*	Apr-05	Dave Johnson, MNDNR	
Bonasa umbellus	Ruffed Grouse	Sibley, 2000	*	May-92	NRRI	

Sandstone Unit of Rice Lake NWR Bird Species List (Continued)

Species		Source	Confirmed	Date	Confirmed by	RCP
Scientific Name	Common Name					
Fulica americana	American Coot	Sibley, 2000				
Rallus limicola	Virginia Rail	Sibley, 2000	*	May-92	NRRI	
Porzana carolina	Sora	Sibley, 2000	*	May-92	NRRI	
Coturnicops noveboracensis	Yellow Rail	Sibley, 2000				*
Grus canadensis	Sandhill Crane (Greater)	Sibley, 2000				
Pluvialis squatarola	Black-bellied Plover	Sibley, 2000				
Pluvialis dominica	American Golden-Plover	Sibley, 2000				
Charadrius semipalmatus	Semipalmated Plover	Sibley, 2000				
Charadrius vociferus	Killdeer	Sibley, 2000				
Tringa melanoleuca	Greater Yellowlegs	Sibley, 2000				*
Tringa flavipes	Lesser Yellowlegs	Sibley, 2000				
Tringa solitaria	Solitary Sandpiper	Sibley, 2000				
Actitis macularia	Spotted Sandpiper	Sibley, 2000				
Limosa haemastica	Hudsonian Godwit	Janssen, 1987				*
Limosa fedoa	Marbled Godwit	Sibley, 2000				*
Bartramia longicauda	Upland Sandpiper	Sibley, 2000				*
Numenius phaeopus	Whimbrel	Janssen, 1987				*
Arenaria interpres	Ruddy Turnstone	Sibley, 2000				
Calidris alba	Sanderling	Sibley, 2000				
Calidris alpina	Dunlin	Sibley, 2000				
Calidris melanotos	Pectoral Sandpiper	Sibley, 2000				
Calidris fuscicollis	White-rumped Sandpiper	Sibley, 2000				
Calidris pusilla	Semipalmated Sandpiper	Sibley, 2000				
Calidris minutilla	Least Sandpiper	Sibley, 2000				
Calidris himantopus	Stilt Sandpiper	Sibley, 2000				*
Limnodromus scolopaceus	Long-billed Dowitcher	Sibley, 2000				
Limnodromus griseus	Short-billed Dowitcher	Sibley, 2000				*
Tryngites subruficollis	Buff-breasted Sandpiper	Janssen, 1987				*
Scolopax minor	American Woodcock	Sibley, 2000				*

Sandstone Unit of Rice Lake NWR Bird Species List (Continued)

Species		Source	Confirmed	Date	Confirmed by	RCP
Scientific Name	**Common Name**					
Gallinago gallinago	Common Snipe	Sibley, 2000				
Phalaropus tricolor	Wilson's Phalarope	Sibley, 2000				*
Phalaropus lobatus	Red-necked Phalarope	Sibley, 2000				
Larus philadephia	Bonaparte's Gull	Sibley, 2000				
Larus pipixcan	Franklin's Gull	Sibley, 2000				
Larus delawarensis	Ring-billed Gull	Sibley, 2000				
Larus argentatus	Herring Gull	Sibley, 2000				
Sterna caspia	Caspian Tern	Sibley, 2000				
Sterna hirundo	Common Tern	Sibley, 2000				*
Sterna forsteri	Forster's Tern	Sibley, 2000				*
Chlidonias niger	Black Tern	Sibley, 2000				*
Zenaida macroura	Mourning Dove	Sibley, 2000				
Coccyzus americanus	Yellow-billed Cuckoo	Sibley, 2000	*	May-92	NRRI	
Coccyzus erythropthalmus	Black-billed Cuckoo	Sibley, 2000	*	May-92	NRRI	*
Asio otus	Long-eared Owl	Sibley, 2000				*
Asio flammeus	Short-eared Owl	Sibley, 2000				*
Bubo virginianus	Great-horned Owl	Sibley, 2000				
Nyctea scandiaca	Snowy Owl	Sibley, 2000				
Strix nebulosa	Great Gray Owl	Sibley, 2000				
Strix varia	Barred Owl	Sibley, 2000				
Aegolius funereus	Boreal Owl	Sibley, 2000				
Aegolius acadicus	Northern Saw-whet Owl	Sibley, 2000				
Otus asio	Eastern Screech-Owl	Sibley, 2000				
Surnia ulula	Northern Hawk Owl	Sibley, 2000				
Caprimalgus vociferus	Whip-poor-will	Sibley, 2000				*
Chordeiles minor	Common Nighthawk	Sibley, 2000				
Chaetura pelagica	Chimney Swift	Sibley, 2000				
Archilochus colubris	Ruby-throated Hummingbird	Sibley, 2000				
Ceryle alcyon	Belted Kingfisher	Sibley, 2000	*	May-92	NRRI	

Sandstone Unit of Rice Lake NWR Bird Species List (Continued)

Species						
Scientific Name	Common Name	Source	Confirmed	Date	Confirmed by	RCP
Melanerpes erythrocephalus	Red-headed Woodpecker	Sibley, 2000				*
Melanerpes carolinus	Red-bellied Woodpecker	Sibley, 2000				
Sphyrapicus varius	Yellow-bellied Sapsucker	Sibley, 2000	*	May-92	NRRI	
Picoides pubescens	Downy Woodpecker	Sibley, 2000	*	May-92	NRRI	
Picoides villosus	Hairy Woodpecker	Sibley, 2000	*	May-92	NRRI	
Picoides arcticus	Black-backed Woodpecker	Sibley, 2000				
Colaptes auratus	Northern Flicker	Sibley, 2000	*	Jul-92	NRRI	*
Dryocopus pileatus	Pileated Woodpecker	Sibley, 2000	*	3/25/04	M. McDowell	
Contopus cooperi	Olive-sided Flycatcher	Sibley, 2000	*	Jun-92	NRRI	*
Contopus virens	Eastern Wood-Pewee	Sibley, 2000	*	May-92	NRRI	
Empidonax flaviventris	Yellow-bellied Flycatcher	Sibley, 2000				
Empidonax alnorum	Alder Flycatcher	Sibley, 2000	*	Jun-92	NRRI	
Empidonax minimus	Least Flycatcher	Sibley, 2000	*	May-92	NRRI	
Sayornis phoebe	Eastern Phoebe	Sibley, 2000	*	May-92	NRRI	
Myiarchus crinitus	Great Crested Flycatcher	Sibley, 2000	*	May-92	NRRI	
Tyrannus tyrannus	Eastern Kingbird	Sibley, 2000	*	May-92	NRRI	
Tyrannus verticalis	Western Kingbird	Sibley, 2000				
Lanius excubitor	Northern Shrike	Sibley, 2000				
Vireo olivaceus	Red-eyed Vireo	Sibley, 2000	*	May-92	NRRI	
Vireo gilvus	Warbling Vireo	Sibley, 2000				
Vireo philadelphicus	Philadelphia Vireo	Sibley, 2000				
Vireo flavifrons	Yellow-throated Vireo	Sibley, 2000	*	Jun-92	NRRI	
Vireo solitarius	Blue-headed Vireo	Sibley, 2000	*	Jul-92	NRRI	
Cyanocitta cristata	Blue Jay	Sibley, 2000	*	3/25/04	M. McDowell	
Perisoreus canadensis	Gray Jay	Sibley, 2000				
Pica hudsonia	Black-billed Magpie	Sibley, 2000				
Corvus corax	Common Raven	Sibley, 2000				
Corvus brachyrhynchos	American Crow	Sibley, 2000	*	3/25/04	M. McDowell	
Eremophila alpestris	Horned Lark	Sibley, 2000				

Sandstone Unit of Rice Lake NWR Bird Species List (Continued)

Species		Source	Confirmed	Date	Confirmed by	RCP
Scientific Name	Common Name					
Progne subis	Purple Martin	Sibley, 2000				
Stelgiopteryx serripennis	Northern Rough-winged Swallow	Sibley, 2000				
Riparia riparia	Bank Swallow	Sibley, 2000				
Tachycineta bicolor	Tree Swallow	Sibley, 2000				
Petrochelidon pyrrhonota	Cliff Swallow	Sibley, 2000				
Hirundo rustica	Barn Swallow	Sibley, 2000	*	Jun-92	NRRI	
Poecile atricapilla	Black-capped Chickadee	Sibley, 2000	*	3/25/04	M. McDowell	
Poecile hudsonica	Boreal Chickadee	Sibley, 2000				
Sitta canadensis	Red-breasted Nuthatch	Sibley, 2000				
Sitta carolinensis	White-breasted Nuthatch	Sibley, 2000	*	May-92	NRRI	
Certhia americana	Brown Creeper	Sibley, 2000	*	May-92	NRRI	
Troglodytes aedon	House Wren	Sibley, 2000	*	Jun-92	NRRI	
Troglodytes troglodytes	Winter Wren	Sibley, 2000	*	May-92	NRRI	
Cistrothorus platensis	Sedge Wren	Sibley, 2000	*	May-92	NRRI	*
Cistothorus palustris	Marsh Wren	Sibley, 2000	*	May-92	NRRI	
Regulus satrapa	Golden-crowned Kinglet	Sibley, 2000				
Reugus calendula	Ruby-crowned Kinglet	Sibley, 2000	*	3/25/04	M. McDowell	
Sialia sialis	Eastern Bluebird	Sibley, 2000	*	Jul-92	NRRI	
Turdus migratorius	American Robin	Sibley, 2000	*	3/25/04	M. McDowell	
Hylocichla mustelina	Wood Thrush	Sibley, 2000	*	May-92	NRRI	*
Catharus fuscescens	Veery	Sibley, 2000	*	May-92	NRRI	
Catharus ustulatus	Swainson's Thrush	Sibley, 2000				
Catharus minimus	Gray-cheeked Thrush	Sibley, 2000				
Catharus guttatus	Hermit Thrush	Sibley, 2000	*	Jul-92	NRRI	
Dumetella carolinensis	Gray Catbird	Sibley, 2000	*	May-92	NRRI	
Toxostoma rufum	Brown Thrasher	Sibley, 2000				
Sturnus vulgaris	European Starling	Sibley, 2000				
Anthus rubescens	American Pipit	Sibley, 2000				

Sandstone Unit of Rice Lake NWR Bird Species List (Continued)

Species						
Scientific Name	Common Name	Source	Confirmed	Date	Confirmed by	RCP
Bombycilla garrulus	Bohemian Waxwing	Sibley, 2000				
Bombycilla cedrorum	Cedar Waxwing	Sibley, 2000	*	Jun-92	NRRI	
Parula americana	Northern Parula	Sibley, 2000				
Vermivora celata	Orange-crowned Warbler	Sibley, 2000				
Vermivora peregrina	Tennessee Warbler	Sibley, 2000	*	May-92	NRRI	
Vermivora chrysoptera	Golden-winged Warbler	Sibley, 2000	*	May-92	NRRI	*
Vermivora ruficapilla	Nashville Warbler	Sibley, 2000	*	May-92	NRRI	
Dendroica petechia	Yellow Warbler	Sibley, 2000	*	May-92	NRRI	
Dendrioca pensylvanica	Chestnut-sided Warbler	Sibley, 2000	*	May-92	NRRI	
Dendrioca magnolia	Magnolia Warbler	Sibley, 2000	*	Jun-92	NRRI	
Dendrioca tigrina	Cape May Warbler	Sibley, 2000				
Dendroica fusca	Blackburnian Warbler	Sibley, 2000	*	May-92	NRRI	
Dendroica coronata	Yellow-rumped Warbler	Sibley, 2000	*	May-92	NRRI	
Dendroica virens	Black-throated Green Warbler	Sibley, 2000				
Dendroica palmarum	Palm Warbler	Sibley, 2000				
Dendroica pinus	Pine Warbler	Sibley, 2000				
Dendroica castanea	Bay-breasted Warbler	Sibley, 2000				
Dendroica striata	Blackpoll Warbler	Sibley, 2000				
Mniotilta varia	Balck-and-white Warbler	Sibley, 2000	*	May-92	NRRI	
Setophaga ruticilla	American Redstart	Sibley, 2000	*	May-92	NRRI	
Seiurus aurocapillus	Ovenbird	Sibley, 2000	*	May-92	NRRI	
Seiurus noveboracensis	Northern Waterthrush	Sibley, 2000	*	May-92	NRRI	
Seiurus motacilla	Louisiana Waterthrush	Sibley, 2000				*
Oporornis agilis	Connecticut Warbler	Sibley, 2000				*
Oporornis philadelphia	Mourning Warbler	Sibley, 2000	*	May-92	NRRI	
Geothlypis trichas	Common Yellowthroat	Sibley, 2000	*	May-92	NRRI	
Wilsonia pusilla	Wilson's Warbler	Sibley, 2000				
Wilsonia canadensis	Canada Warbler	Sibley, 2000	*	May-92	NRRI	*
Piranga olivacea	Scarlet Tanager	Sibley, 2000	*	May-92	NRRI	

Sandstone Unit of Rice Lake NWR Bird Species List (Continued)

Species		Source	Confirmed	Date	Confirmed by	RCP
Scientific Name	Common Name					
Cardinalis cardinalis	Northern Cardinal	Sibley, 2000				
Pheucticus ludovicianus	Rose-breasted Grosbeak	Sibley, 2000	*	May-92	NRRI	
Passerina cyanea	Indigo Bunting	Sibley, 2000	*	Jul-92	NRRI	
Pipilo erythrophthalmus	Eastern Towhee	Sibley, 2000	*	May-92	NRRI	
Spizella arborea	American Tree Sparrow	Sibley, 2000				
Spizella pusilla	Field Sparrow	Sibley, 2000				*
Spizella pallida	Clay-colored Sparrow	Sibley, 2000	*	May-92	NRRI	
Spizella passerina	Chipping Sparrow	Sibley, 2000	*	May-92	NRRI	
Ammodramus savannarum	Grasshopper Sparrow	Sibley, 2000				*
Ammodramus leconteii	Le Conte's Sparrow	Sibley, 2000				*
Passerculus sandwichensis	Savannah Sparrow	Sibley, 2000	*	May-92	NRRI	
Pooecetes gramineus	Vesper Sparrow	Sibley, 2000	*	Jul-92	NRRI	
Zonotrichia querula	Harris's Sparrow	Sibley, 2000				
Zonotrichia albicollis	White-throated Sparrow	Sibley, 2000	*	Jul-92	NRRI	
Zonotrichia leucophrys	White-crowned Sparrow	Sibley, 2000				
Passerella iliaca	Fox Sparrow	Sibley, 2000				
Melospiza melodia	Song Sparrow	Sibley, 2000	*	May-92	NRRI	
Melospiza lincolnii	Lincoln's Sparrow	Sibley, 2000				
Melospiza georgiana	Swamp Sparrow	Sibley, 2000	*	May-92	NRRI	
Junco hyemalis	Dark-eyed Junco	Sibley, 2000				
Calcarius pictus	Smith's Longspur	Sibley, 2000				
Calcarius lapponicus	Lapland Longspur	Sibley, 2000				
Plectrophenax nivalis	Snow Bunting	Sibley, 2000				
Sturnella neglecta	Western Meadowlark	Sibley, 2000				*
Sturnella magna	Eastern Meadowlark	Sibley, 2000	*	May-92	NRRI	*
Dolichonyx oryzivorus	Bobolink	Sibley, 2000	*	May-92	NRRI	*
Molothrus ater	Brown-headed Cowbird	Sibley, 2000	*	May-92	NRRI	
Xanthocephalus xanthocephalus	Yellow-headed Blackbird	Sibley, 2000				
Agelaius phoeniceus	Red-winged Blackbird	Sibley, 2000	*	May-92	NRRI	

Sandstone Unit of Rice Lake NWR Bird Species List (Continued)

Species						
Scientific Name	Common Name	Source	Confirmed	Date	Confirmed by	RCP
Euphagus cyanocephalus	Brewer's Blackbird	Sibley, 2000				
Euphagus carolinus	Rusty Blackbird	Sibley, 2000				
Quiscalus quiscula	Common Grackle	Sibley, 2000	*	May-92	NRRI	
Icterus galbula	Baltimore Oriole	Sibley, 2000	*	May-92	NRRI	
Icterus spurius	Orchard Oriole	Sibley, 2000				*
Coccothraustes vespertinus	Evening Grosbeak	Sibley, 2000				
Pinicola enucleator	Pine Grosbeak	Sibley, 2000				
Carpodacus purpureus	Purple Finch	Sibley, 2000	*	Jun-92	NRRI	
Carpodacus mexicanus	House Finch	Sibley, 2000				
Loxia curvirostra	Red Crossbill	Sibley, 2000				
Loxia leucoptera	White-winged Crossbill	Sibley, 2000				
Carduelis flammea	Common Redpoll	Sibley, 2000				
Carduelis hornemanni	Hoary Redpoll	Sibley, 2000				
Carduelis pinus	Pine Siskin	Sibley, 2000				
Caruelis tristis	American Goldfinch	Sibley, 2000	*	May-92	NRRI	
Passer domesticus	House Sparrow	Sibley, 2000				

Literature Cited
Sibley, D. 2000. National Audubon Society The Sibley Guide to Birds. Alfred A. Knopf, Inc. New York. 544 pp.
Janssen, R. 1987. Birds in Minnesota. University of Minnesota. Minneapolis, Minnesota. 352 pp.
NRRI = Natural Resources Reseach Institute, University of Minnesota, Duluth

Rice Lake NWR Tree and Shrub Species List

Species						
Scientific Name	Common Name	Native	Source	Confirmed	Date	Confirmed by
Abies balsamea	Balsam fir	Y	Weeks et al. 2005	*	Oct-96	D. King
Picea glauca	White spruce	Y	Weeks et al. 2005	*	3/10/95	R. Lloyd
Picea mariana	Black spruce	Y	Weeks et al. 2005	*	12/30/97	W. Brininger, R. Lloyd
Picea pungens	Blue spruce	N	Weeks et al. 2005	*	6/1/04	M. McDowell
Pinus banksiana	Jack pine	Y	Weeks et al. 2005	*	Mar-98	D. King
Pinus resinosa	Red pine, Norway pine	Y	Weeks et al. 2005	*	3/14/95	R. Lloyd
Pinus strobus	Eastern white pine	Y	Weeks et al. 2005	*	3/14/95	R. Lloyd
Thuja occindentalis	Northern white-cedar	Y	Weeks et al. 2005	*	2/14/97	W. Brininger, R. Lloyd
Larix laricina	Tamarack, Eastern larch	Y	Weeks et al. 2005	*	12/30/97	W. Brininger, R. Lloyd
Acer rubrum	Red maple	Y	Weeks et al. 2005	*	1/22/98	W. Brininger
Acer saccharinum	Silver maple	Y	Weeks et al. 2005	*	Jun-96	C. Kasper
Acer saccharum	Sugar maple	Y	Weeks et al. 2005	*	Oct-97	D. King
Acer spicatum	Mountain maple	Y	Tester 1995	*	10/15/96	D. King
Acer neguno	Boxelder	Y	Weeks et al. 2005			
Fraxinus nigra	Black ash	Y	Weeks et al. 2005	*	2/14/97	W. Brininger, R. Lloyd
Fraxinus pennsylvanica	Green ash	Y	Weeks et al. 2005	*	Oct-96	D. King
Amelanchier arborea	Downy serviceberry, Juneberry	Y	Weeks et al. 2005	*	1995	D. King, R. Lloyd
Amelanchier sanguinea	Roundleaf serviceberry	Y	Tekiela 2001			
Betula alleghaniensis	Yellow birch	Y	Weeks et al. 2005	*	4/29/97	W. Brininger, R. Lloyd
Betula papyrifera	Paper birch	Y	Weeks et al. 2005	*	Oct-96	D. King
Ostrya virginiana	Eastern hophornbeam, Ironwood	Y	Weeks et al. 2005	*	9/20/95	R. Lloyd
Populus balsamifera	Balsam poplar, Balm of Gilead	Y	Weeks et al. 2005	*	2/14/97	W. Brininger, R. Lloyd
Populus gradidentata	Bigtooth aspen	Y	Weeks et al. 2005	*	May-94	D. King, R. Lloyd

Rice Lake NWR Tree and Shrub Species List (Continued)

Scientific Name	Common Name	Native	Source	Confirmed	Date	Confirmed by
Populus tremuloides	Quaking aspen	Y	Weeks et al. 2005	*	2/14/97	W. Brininger, R. Lloyd
Prunus americana	American plum	N (Y in MN, not Aitkin Co.)		*	6/1/04	M. McDowell
Prunus pensylvanica	Pin cherry	Y	Weeks et al. 2005			
Prunus serotina	Black cherry	Y	Weeks et al. 2005			
Prunus virginiana	Choke cherry	Y	Tester 1995	*	9/18/95	D. King, R. Lloyd
Quercus ellipsoidalis	Northern pin oak	Y	Weeks et al. 2005			
Quercus macrocarpa	Bur oak	Y	Weeks et al. 2005	*	1/22/98	W. Brininger
Quercus rubra	Northern red oak	Y	Weeks et al. 2005	*	1/22/98	W. Brininger
Tilia americana	American basswood	Y	Weeks et al. 2005	*	Oct-96	D. King
Ulmus americana	American elm	Y	Weeks et al. 2005	*	Apr-96	C. Kasper
Ulmus thomasii	Rock elm	Y	Weeks et al. 2005	*	1995	R. Lloyd
Juglans cinerea	White walnut, Butternut, Butternut hickory	Y	Weeks et al. 2005	*	Oct-97	D. King
Viburnum lentago	Nannyberry	Y	Tekiela 2001	*	9/15/06	M. McDowell
Viburnum trilobum	High-bush cranberry	Y	Tester 1995			
Viburnum recognitum	Arrowwood	Y	Newcomb 1977	*	Apr-96	C. Kasper
Viburnum rafinesquianum	Downy arrow-wood	Y	Tester 1995			
Salix discolor	Pussy willow	Y	Tekiela 2001	*	1/22/98	W. Brininger
Alnus rugosa	Speckled alder	Y	Tekiela 2001	*	1/22/98	W. Brininger
Vaccinium angustifolium	Lowbush blueberry	Y	Tester 1995	*	4/1/98	D. King
Betula pumila	Bog birch	Y	Tester 1995			
Kalmia polifolia	Bog laurel	Y	Tester 1995			
Andromeda glaucophylla	Bog rosemary	Y	Tester 1995	*	12/30/97	W. Brininger, R. Lloyd
Ribes sp.	Current, Gooseberry	Y	Tester 1995			
Cornus alternifolia	Pagoda dogwood	Y	Tester 1995			

Rice Lake NWR Tree and Shrub Species List (Continued)

Scientific Name	Common Name	Native	Source	Confirmed	Date	Confirmed by
Cornus stolonifera	Red osier dogwood	Y	Tester 1995	*	12/18/97	W. Brininger, R. Lloyd
Sambucus canadensis	Common elder	Y	Tester 1995	*	1/1/98	W. Brininger, R. Lloyd
Sambucus pubens	Red-berried elder	Y	Tester 1995			
Ledum groenlandicum	Labrador tea	Y	Tester 1995	*	12/30/97	W. Brininger, R. Lloyd
Chamaedaphne calyculata	Leather-leaf	Y	Tester 1995	*	12/30/97	W. Brininger, R. Lloyd
Physocarpus opulifolius	Ninebark	Y	Tester 1995			
Rosa blanda	Wild rose	Y	Tester 1995	*	4/1/97	D. King
Rubus sp.	Raspberry	Y	Tester 1995	*	9/1/96	D. King, R. Lloyd
Zanthoxylum americanum	Prickly ash	Y	Tester 1995			
Spiraea alba	Spirea	Y	Tester 1995			
Rhus vernix	Poison sumac	Y	Tester 1995			
Rhus glabra	Smooth sumac	Y	Tester 1995			
Rhus typhina	Staghorn sumac	Y	Tester 1995	*	1/1/98	W. Brininger, R. Lloyd
Ilex verticillata	Winterberry	Y	Tester 1995			
Gaultheria procumbens	Wintergreen	Y	Tester 1995			
Symphoricarpos occidentalis	Wolfberry	Y	Tester 1995			
Corylus americana	American hazelnut	Y	Tester 1995			
Corylus cornuta	Beaked hazelnut	Y	Tester 1995	*	9/1/96	D. King, R. Lloyd
Diervilla lonicera	Bush honeysuckle	Y	Tester 1995			
Lonicera canadensis	Fly honeysuckle	Y	Tester 1995			
Lonicera villosa	Northern honeysuckle, Mountain fly honeysuckle	Y	Petrides 1972, Newcomb 1977			
Cratagus sp.	Hawthorn	Y	Newcomb 1977	*	1/1/98	W. Brininger, R. Lloyd
Syringa vulgaris	Common Lilac	N	Petrides 1972	*	7/9/97	D. King

Rice Lake NWR Tree and Shrub Species List (Continued)

Species					
Scientific Name	**Common Name**	**Native**	**Source**	**Confirmed**	**Date**	**Confirmed by**

Literature Cited:

Newcomb, Lawrence. 1977. Newcomb's wildflower guide. Little Brown and Company, Boston, New York, London. 490 Pages.

Tekiela, Stan. 2001. Trees of Minnesota field guide. Adventure Publications Inc., Cambridge, Minnesota. 193 Pages.

Tester, John R. 1995. Minnesota's natural heritage. University of Minnesota Press. Minneapolis, Minnesota. 332 Pages.

Petrides, George A. 1972. The Peterson field guide series: a field guide to trees and shrubs. Second Edition. Houghton Mifflin Company. Boston, Massachusetts. 428 Pages.

Weeks, Sally S., Harmon P. Weeks, Jr., George R. Parker. 2005. Native trees of the Midwest: identification, wildlife values, and landscaping use. Purdue University Press, West Lafayette, Indiana. 325 Pages.

Vegetation Species List, Rice Lake NWR[1]

Common Name	Genus	Species	Family	Sp_Code	P_A_B	Native	Life Form	Color
Yellow goatsbeard	Tragopogon	*dubius Scop.*	Asteraceae	TRDU1	B	N	Forb	yellow
Virginia water-leaf	Hydrophyllum	*virginianum L.*	Hydrophyllaceae	HYVI1	P	Y	Forb	purple
Steeplebush	Spiraea	*tomentosa*	Rosaceae	SPTO1	P	Y	Shrub	rose-purp
Grey dogwood	Cornus	*racemosa Lam.*	Cornaceae	CORA1	P	Y	Shrub	white
Purple Loosestrife	Lythrum	*salicaria*	Lythraceae	LYSA1	P	N	Forb	purple
Wild Cucumber	Echinocystis	*lobata*	Cucurbitaceae	ECLO1	A	Y	Forb	green/whi
Motherwort	Leonurus	*cardiaca*	Libiatae	LECA1	P	N	Forb	pale purp
Yellow Violet	Viola	*pubescens Ait.*	Violacaea	VIPU1	P	Y	Forb	yellow
Narrow-leaved Meadowsweet	Spiraea	*alba*	Rosaceae	SPAL1	P	Y	Shrub	white
Steeplebush	Spiraea	*tomentosa*	Rosaceae	SPTO1	P	Y	Shrub	white/pin
Pickerel Weed	Pontederia	*cordata L.*	Pontederiaceae	POCO1	P	Y	Forb	purple
Pond Lily	Nuphar	*advena L.*	Pontederiaceae	NUAD1	P	Y	Forb	yellow
Hard-stem Bulrush	Scirpus	*acutus*	Cyperaceae	SCAC1	P	Y	Sedge	non-flowe
Dame's rocket	Hesperis	*matronalis L.*	Brassicaceae	HEMA1	B	N	Forb	purple
Bird's-foot trefoil	Lotus	*corniculatus L.*	Fabaceae	LOCO1	P	N	Forb	yellow
Water Plantain	Alisma	*sp.*	Alismataceae	ALSP1	P	Y	Forb	white
Broad-leaved Arrowhead	Sagittaria	*latifolia Willd.*	Anacardiaceae	SALA1	P	Y	Forb	white
Staghorn Sumac	Rhus	*typhina*	Anacardiaceae	RHTY1	P	Y	Shrub	red
Water Hemlock	Cicuta	*maculata*	Apiaceae	CIMA1	P	Y	Forb	white

Vegetation Species List, Rice Lake NWR[1] (Continued)

Common Name	Genus	Species	Family	Sp_Code	P_A_B	Native	Life Form	Color
Cow Parsnip	Heracleum	*lanatum*	Apiaceae	HELA1	P	Y	Forb	white/yel
Bland Sweet Cicely	Osmorhiza	*claytonii (Michx.) C.*	Apiaceae	OSCL1	P	Y	Forb	nonflower
Black Snakeroot	Sanicula	*marilandica L.*	Apiaceae	SAMA1	P	Y	Forb	greenish
Spreading Dogbane	Apocynum	*androsaemifolium*	Apocynaceae	APAN1	P	Y	Forb	pink/whit
Calla Lily	Calla	*palustris*	Araceae	CAPA1	P	Y	Forb	white
American Spikenard	Aralia	*racemosa*	Araliaceae	ARRA1	P	Y	Forb	white
Swamp Milkweed	Asclepias	*incarnata*	Asclepiadaceae	ASIN1	P	Y	Forb	rose purp
Common Milkweed	Asclepias	*syriaca*	Asclepiadaceae	ASSY1	P	Y	Forb	pink
Maidenhair Fern	Adiatum	*pedatum*	Aspleniaceae	ADPE1	P	Y	Fern	non-flowe
Lady Fern	Athyrium	*felix-femina*	Aspleniaceae	ATFE1	P	Y	Fern	non-flowe
Common Yarrow	Achillea	*millefolium*	Asteraceae	ACMI1	P	Y	Forb	white
Field Pussytoes	Antennaria	*neglecta*	Asteraceae	ANNE1	P	Y	Forb	white
Flat-topped Aster	Aster	*umbellatus*	Asteraceae	ASUM1	P	Y	Forb	white
Ox-eye Daisy	Chrysanthemum	*leucanthemum*	Asteraceae	CHLE1	P	N	Forb	white
Canada Thistle	Cirsium	*arvense*	Asteraceae	CIAR1	P	N	Forb	purple
Horseweed	Conyza	*canadensis*	Asteraceae	COCA1	A	Y	Forb	white
Large-flowered Coreopsis	Coreopsis	*sp.*	Asteraceae	COSP1	A	N	Forb	orange
Plain's Coreopsis	Coreopsis	*tinctoria*	Asteraceae	COTI1	A	Y	Forb	maroon/ye
NarrowLeaved Hawk's beard	Crepis	*tectorum*	Asteraceae	CRTE1	A	Y	Forb	yellow
Prarie Coneflower	Echinacea	*pallida Nutt.*	Asteraceae	ECPA1	P	Y	Forb	yellow

Vegetation Species List, Rice Lake NWR[1] (Continued)

Common Name	Genus	Species	Family	Sp_Code	P_A_B	Native	Life Form	Color
Philidelphia Daisy	Erigeron	*philidelphicus*	Asteraceae	ERPH1	B/P	Y	Forb	white/pin
Rough Fleabane	Erigeron	*strigosus*	Asteraceae	ERST1	A/B	Y	Forb	white/pin
Blanket Flower	Gaillardia	*pulchella*	Asteraceae	GAPU1	A	Y	Forb	maroon/ye
Swamp Sunflower	Helianthus	*giganteus*	Asteraceae	HEGI1	P	Y	Forb	yellow
Ox-eye	Heliopsis	*helianthoides*	Asteraceae	HEHE1	P	Y	Forb	yellow
Orange Hawkweed	Hieracium	*aurantiacum*	Asteraceae	HIAU1	P	N	Forb	orange re
Canada Lettuce	Lactuca	*canadensis*	Asteraceae	LACA1	B	Y	Forb	white
Pineapple Weed	Matricaria	*matricarioides*	Asteraceae	MAMA1	A	Y	Forb	yellow
Columnar Coneflower	Ratibida	*columnifera*	Asteraceae	RACO1	P	Y	Forb	maroon
Black-eyed Susan	Rudbeckia	*hirta*	Asteraceae	RUHI1	B	Y	Forb	yellow
Green-headed Coneflower	Rudbeckia	*laciniata*	Asteraceae	RULA1	P	Y	Forb	yellow
Balsam Ragwort	Senecio	*pauperculus*	Asteraceae	SEPA1	P	Y	Forb	yellow
Whooly Ragwort	Senecio	*tomentosus*	Asteraceae	SETO1	P	N	Forb	yellow
Early Goldenrod	Solidago	*juncea Aiton.*	Asteraceae	SOJU1	P	Y	Forb	yellow
Bog Goldenrod	Solidago	*uliginosa Nutt.*	Asteraceae	SOUL1	P	Y	Forb	yellow
Common Cow Thistle	Sonchus	*oleraceus L.*	Asteraceae	SOOL1	A	N	Forb	yellow
Dandelion	Taraxacum	*officinale G.H. Weber*	Asteraceae	TAOF1	P	N	Forb	yellow or
Nutsedge (Flatsedge)	Cyperus	*sp.*	Cyperaceae	CYSP1	P	Y	Sedge	non-flowe

Vegetation Species List, Rice Lake NWR[1] (Continued)

Common Name	Genus	Species	Family	Sp_Code	P_A_B	Native	Life Form	Color
Spotted Touch-me-not (Jew	Impatiens	*capensis Meerb.*	Balsaminaceae	IMCA1	A	Y	Forb	yellow
Hornbeam	Ostrya	*virginiana (P.Mill) K.*	Betulaceae	OSVI1	P	Y	Tree/shru	white
Hoary Alyssum	Berteroa	*incana*	Brassicaceae	BEIN1	P	N	Forb	white/yel
Brown Mustard	Brassica	*juncea*	Brassicaceae	BRJU1	A	N	Forb	yellow
Showy Tick Trefoil	Desmodium	*canadense*	Leguminosae	DECA1	P	Y	Forb	rose-purp
Marsh Bellflower	Campanula	*aparinoides*	Brassicaceae	CAAP1	P	Y	Forb	white/pal
Northern Bush Honeysuckle	Diervilla	*lonicera*	Caprifoliaceae	DILO1	P	Y	Shrub	yellow
Trumpet Honeysuckle	Lonicera	*sempervirens L.*	Caprifoliaceae	LOSE1	P	Y	Forb	red/yello
Common Elderberry	Sambucus	*canadensis L.*	Caprifoliaceae	SACA1	P	Y	Shrub	red
Nannyberry	Viburnum	*lentago L.*	Caprifoliaceae	VILE1	P	Y	Shrub	white
Highbush Cranberry	Viburnum	*trilobum*	Caprifoliaceae	VITR1	P	Y	Shrub	white
Deptford Pink	Dianthus	*armeria*	Caryophyllaceae	DIAR1	A	N	Forb	red
Sweet William Catchfly	Silene	*armeria L.*	Caryophyllaceae	SIAR1	A	N	Forb	purple
White Cockle	Silene	*latifolia Poir.*	Caryophyllaceae	SILA1	A	N	Forb	white
Hedge Bindweed	Convolvulus	*sepium*	Convolvulaceae	COSE1	P	Y/N	Forb	pink/whit
Alternate-leaved Dogwood	Cornus	*alternifolia*	Cornaceae	COAL1	P	Y	Shrub	non-flowe

Vegetation Species List, Rice Lake NWR[1] (Continued)

Common Name	Genus	Species	Family	Sp_Code	P_A_B	Native	Life Form	Color
Poor-man's Pepper-grass	Lepidium	*virginicum*	Brassicaceae	LEVI1	A/B	Y	Forb	non-flowe
Black Bulrush	Scirpus	*atrovirens*	Cyperaceae	SCAT1	P	Y	Sedge	green/bro
Wool Grass	Scirpus	*cyperinus (L.) Kunth*	Cyperaceae	SCCY1	P	Y	Sedge	brown
Leafy Spurge	Euphorbia	*esula*	Euphorbiaceae	EUES1	P	N	Forb	yellow
Woodland Horsetail	Equisetum	*sylvaticum*	Equisetaceae	EQSY1	P	Y	Forb	non-flowe
Pointed-leaved Tick-Trefo	Desmodium	*glutinosum*	Fabaceae	DEGL1	P	Y	Forb	pink/purp
Wild Geranium	Geranium	*maculatum*	Geraniaceae	GEMA1	P	Y	Forb	purple
Forest Pea	Lathyrus	*venosus Muhl. ex Wild*	Fabaceae	LAVE1	P	Y	Forb	purple
Spotted Joe-Pye-Weed	Eupatorium	*maculatum L.*	Asteraceae	EUMA1	P	Y	Forb	pink
Alfalfa	Medicago	*sativa L.*	Fabaceae	MESA1	P	N	Forb	purple/bl
Sweet White Clover	Melilotus	*alba White.*	Fabaceae	MEAL1	B	N	Forb	white
Sweet Yellow Clover	Melilotus	*officinalis (L.) Lam*	Fabaceae	MEOF1	B	N	Forb	yellow
Rabbit's Foot Clover	Trifolium	*arvense L.*	Fabaceae	TRAR1	A	N	Forb	pink/gray
Pinnate Hop-clover	Trifolium	*campestre Schreb.*	Fabaceae	TRCA1	A	N	Forb	yellow
Alsike Clover	Trifolium	*hybridum L.*	Fabaceae	TRHY1	P	N	Forb	magenta/w
Red Clover	Trifolium	*patense L.*	Fabaceae	TRPA1	P	N	Forb	magenta
Yellow Hop Clover	Trifolium	*procumbens*	Fabaceae	TRPR1	A	N	Forb	yellow
American Vetch	Vicia	*americana Muhl. ex Wil*	Fabaceae	VIAM1	P	Y	Forb	blue
Cow Vetch	Vicia	*cracca L.*	Fabaceae	VICR1	P	N	Forb	purple/bl

Vegetation Species List, Rice Lake NWR[1] (Continued)

Common Name	Genus	Species	Family	Sp_Code	P_A_B	Native	Life Form	Color
Beck's Water-Marigold	Bidens	*beckii*	Asteraceae	BIBE1	P	Y	Forb	yellow
Pasture Gooseberry	Ribes	*cynosbati L.*	Grossulariaceae	RICY1	P	Y	Shrub	green
Missouri Goldenrod	Solidago	*missouriensis Nutt.*	Asteraceae	SOMI1	P	Y	Forb	yellow
Blue Flag Iris-Larger	Iris	*versicolor*	Iridaceae	IRVE1	P	Y	Forb	purple
Blue-eyed Grass	Sisyrinchium	*macronatum*	Iridaceae	SIMU1	P	Y	Forb	purple
Purple Giant Hyssop	Agastache	*scrophulariaefolia*	Lamiaceae	AGSC1	P	Y	Forb	purple
Wild Mint	Mentha	*arvensis L.*	Lamiaceae	MEAR1	P	Y	Forb	white
Wild Bergamot	Monarda	*fistulosa L.*	Lamiaceae	MOFI1	P	Y	Forb	pink/purp
Heal-all	Prunella	*vulgaris L.*	Lamiaceae	PRVU1	p	Y	Forb	purple
Common Mountain Mint	Pycananthemum	*virginianum (L). T.Dur*	Lamiaceae	PYVI1	P	Y	Forb	white
Marsh Skullcap	Scutellaria	*epilobiifolia*	Lamiaceae	SCEP1	P	Y	Sedge	purple
Hedge-nettle	Stachys	*palustris L.*	Lamiaceae	STPA1	P	Y	Forb	light pur
Greater Bladderwort	Utricularia	*vulgaris L.*	Lentibulariacea	UTVU1	P	Y	Forb	yellow
Day Lily	Hemerocallis	*fulva*	Liliaceae	HEFU1	P	N	Forb	orange
Turk's Cap Lily	Lilium	*superbum L.*	Liliaceae	LISU1	P	Y	Forb	orange
False Solomon's Seal	Smilacina	*racemosa L.*	Liliaceae	SMRA1	P	Y	Forb	white
White Water Lily	Nymphaea	*odorata Ait.*	Nymphaceae	NYOD1	P	Y	Forb	white
Fireweed	Epilobium	*angustifolium*	Onagraceae	EPAN1	P	Y	Forb	magenta

Vegetation Species List, Rice Lake NWR[1] (Continued)

Common Name	Genus	Species	Family	Sp_Code	P_A_B	Native	Life Form	Color
Yellow Evening Primrose	Oenothera	*pilosella Raf.*	Onagraceae	OEPI1	P	Y	Forb	yellow
Sundrops	Oenothera	*tetragona Roth.*	Onagraceae	OETE1	P	Y	Forb	yellow
Sensitive Fern	Onoclea	*sensibilis L.*	Onocleaceae	ONSE1	P	Y	Fern	non-flowe
Purple Fringed Orchid	Habenaria	*psycodes*	Orchidaceae	HAPS1	P	Y	Forb	purple
Large Yellow Lady Slipper	Cypripedium	*calceolus*	Orchidaceae	CYCA1	P	Y	Forb	yellow
Interrupted Fern	Osmunda	*claytoniana L.*	Osmundaceae	OSCL1	P	Y	Fern	non-flowe
Bloodroot	Sanguinaria	*canadensis L.*	Papaveraceae	SACA1	P	Y	Forb	white
Fringed Loosestrife	Lysimachia	*ciliata*	Primulaceae	LYCI1	P	Y	Forb	yellow
Bulbil Loosestrife	Lysimachia	*terrestris (L.) B.S.P.*	Primulaceae	LYTE1	P	Y	Forb	yellow
Pennsylvania Smartweed	Polygonum	*pensylvanicum L.*	Polygonaceae	POPE1	A	Y	Forb	pink
Arrow-leaved Tearthumb	Polygonum	*sagittatum L.*	Polygonaceae	POSA1	A	Y	Forb	white/pin
Red Sorrel	Rumex	*acetosella L.*	Polygonaceae	RUAC1	P	N	Forb	red
Curly Dock	Rumex	*crispus L.*	Polygonaceae	RUCR1	P	N	Forb	green
Western Dock	Rumex	*occidentalis*	Polygonaceae	RUOC1	P	Y	Forb	green/red
Redtop	Agrostis	*gigantea*	Poaceae	AGGI1	P	N	Grass	non-flowe
Fringed Brome	Bromus	*ciliatus*	Poaceae	BRCI1	P	Y	Grass	non-flowe
Smooth Brome	Bromus	*inermis*	Poaceae	BRIN1	P	N	Grass	non-flowe
Orchard Grass	Dactylis	*glomerata*	Poaceae	DAGL1	P	N	Grass	non-flowe

Vegetation Species List, Rice Lake NWR[1] (Continued)

Common Name	Genus	Species	Family	Sp_Code	P_A_B	Native	Life Form	Color
Timothy	Phluem	pratense L.	Poaceae	PHPR11	P	N	Grass	non-flowe
Bog Bluegrass	Poa	paludigena Fern. & Wie	Poaceae	POPA1	P	Y	Grass	non-flowe
Red Baneberry	Actaea	rubra	Ranunculaceae	ACRU1	P	Y	Forb	white
Canada Anemone	Anemone	canadensis	Ranunculaceae	ANCA1	P	Y	Forb	white
Columbine	Aquilegia	canadensis	Ranunculaceae	AQCA1	P	Y	Forb	scarlet/y
Swamp Buttercup	Ranunculus	septentrionalis	Ranunculaceae	RASE1	P	Y	Forb	yellow
Purple Meadow Rue	Thalictrum	dasycarpum Fisch.&Ave-	Ranunculaceae	THDA1	P	Y	Forb	white/pin
Tall Meadow Rue	Thalictrum	pubescens Pursh.	Ranunculaceae	THPU1	P	Y	Forb	white
Canada Goldenrod	Solidago	canadensis L.	Asteraceae	SOCA1	P	Y	Forb	yellow
Roadside Agrimony	Agrimonia	striata	Rosaceae	AGST1	P	Y	Forb	yellow
Yellow Avens	Geum	aleppicum	Rosaceae	GEAL1	P	Y	Forb	yellow
Rough Avens	Geum	laciniatum	Rosaceae	GELA1	P	Y	Forb	yellow
Large-leaved Avens	Geum	macrophyllum	Rosaceae	GEMA1	P	Y	Forb	yellow
Silvery Cinquefoil	Potentilla	argentea L.	Rosaceae	POAR1	P	N	Forb	yellow
Marsh Chinquefoil	Potentilla	palustris (L.) Scop.	Rosaceae	POPA1	P	Y	Forb	red/purpl
Rough Fruited Chinquefoil	Potentilla	recta L.	Rosaceae	PORE1	P	N	Forb	yellow
Old-field Cinquefoil	Potentilla	simplex Michx.	Rosaceae	POSI1	P	Y	Forb	yellow
Western Rose	Rosa	woodsii Lindley.	Rosaceae	ROWO1	P	Y	Shrub	pink
Bristly Blackberry	Rubus	setosus Bigel.	Rosaceae	RUSE1	B/P	Y	Shrub	white
Meadowsweet	Spirea	alba DuRoi	Rosaceae	SPAL1	P	Y	Shrub	white

Vegetation Species List, Rice Lake NWR[1] (Continued)

Common Name	Genus	Species	Family	Sp_Code	P_A_B	Native	Life Form	Color
Rough Bedstraw	Galium	*asprellum Michx.*	Rubiaceae	GAAS1	P	Y	Forb	white
Northern Bedstraw	Galium	*boreale L.*	Rubiaceae	GABO1	P	Y	Forb	white
Bastard Toadflax	Comandra	*umbellata*	Santalaceae	COUM1	P	Y	Forb/ Semi	white
Indian Paintbrush	Castilleja	*coccinea*	Scrophulariacea	CACO1	A	Y	Forb/ Sem	red/orang
Turtle Head	Chelone	*glabra*	Scrophulariacea	CHGL1	P	Y	Forb	white
Butter and Eggs	Linaria	*vulgaris P.Mill*	Scrophulariacea	LIVU1	P	N	Forb	yellow/or
Common Mullein	Verbascum	*thapsus L.*	Scrophulariacea	VETH1	B	N	Forb	yellow
Giant Bur-reed	Sparganium	*eurycarpum Engelm.ex G*	Sparganiaceae	SPEU1	P	Y	Forb	non-flowe
Common Blue Vervain	Verbena	*hastata L.*	Verbenaceae	VEHA1	P	Y	Forb	purple/bl
White Vervain	Verbena	*urticifolia L.*	Verbenaceae	VEUR1	A	Y	Forb	purple/wh
White Baneberry	Actaea	*pachypoda*	Ranunculaceae	ACPA1	P	Y	Forb	white
Thin-leaved Sunflower	Helianthus	*decapetalus*	Asteraceae	HEDE1	P	Y	Forb	yellow
Common Tansy	Tanacetum	*vulgare*	Compositae	TAVU1	P	N	Forb	yellow
Meadow Horsetail	Equisetum	*pratense Ehrh.*	Equisetaceae	EQPR1	A	Y	Fern	non-flowe
Common Ragweed	Ambrosia	*artemisifolia L.*	Asteraceae	AMAR1	A	Y	Forb	green
Western Ragweed	Ambrosia	*psilostachya DC.*	Asteraceae	AMPS1	P	Y	Forb	green
Early Meadow Rue	Thalictrum	*dioicum*	Rannunculaceae	THDI1	p	Y	Forb	white/yel
Horsetail	Equisetum	*sp.*	Equisetaceae	EQSP1	A/P	Y	Forb	non-flowe

Vegetation Species List, Rice Lake NWR[1] (Continued)

Common Name	Genus	Species	Family	Sp_Code	P_A_B	Native	Life Form	Color
Nodding Trillium	Trillium	*cernuum*	Liliaceae	TRCE1	P	Y	Forb	white
Panicled Dogwood	Cornus	*racemosa*	Cornaceae	CORA1	P	Y	Shrub	white

1. *Derived from herbarium inventory only.*
2) *P: perennial; A: annual; B: biannual.*

Appendix E: Rice Lake NWR Biological Surveys

Biological Surveys, Rice Lake NWR

Study/Survey	Priority(10 high, 1 low)	CCP Objective	Scales	FWS R3 RCP	# Runs	# Routes
Ring-necked Duck Post-Fledgling Refuge Use	10		Refuge, State		NA	NA
Water Level Monitoring	10	2.2	Refuge		36	1
Invasive Plant Species Monitoring and Mapping	10	1.9	Refuge, State, National		NA	NA
Invasive Invertebrate Monitoring	10	1.8	Refuge, State		NA	NA
Forest Inventory Assessment	10	1.1, 1.2, 1.3, 1.4, 2.2	Refuge, State, Region		NA	NA
Common Tern Production (Mille Lacs NWR)	9	2.1, 2.2, 6.1	Refuge, State	X	12	1
Wild Rice Bed Area (GIS, georectifying aerial photos)	9	1.8, 2.2	Refuge		1	1
Fall Waterfowl Surveys	8	2.1, 2.2	Refuge, State, Mississippi Flyway	X	16	3
Wild Rice Density/Productivity	8	1.8, 2.2	Refuge, N. MN		1	4
Double Crested Cormorant Production (Mille Lacs NWR)	8	2.1, 6.2, 2.2	Refuge, State	X	1	1
Pickerelweed 10 acre Mowing Study, Phase II	8	1.7	Refuge, MN, WI, MI		NA	NA
Water Quality Monitoring	8	2.2	Refuge		16	1
Prescribed Burn Effects Monitoring	8	1.6, 2.2	Refuge		NA	NA
Fish Trapping Program and Monitoring Invasive Fish	8	1.8	Refuge, State		NA	NA
Weather Monitoring	8		Refuge, State, National		NA	NA
Pickerelweed Mowing Study, Phase I	7	1.7	Refuge, MN, WI, MI		NA	NA
National Marsh Bird Monitoring and Research Program	7	2.1, 2.2	Refuge, National	X	3	3
National American Woodcock Singing Ground Survey	7	2.2	National	X	1	3
Species Lists	7	2.1	Refuge	X	NA	NA
White Pine Restoration - Locations, Phase I	6	1.2	Refuge, State		NA	NA
Nongame Landbird Point Counts, Forest	6	2.1, 2.2	Refuge, National	X	NA	NA
Waterfowl Breeding Pair Survey	5	2.1, 2.2	Refuge	X	1	3
Waterfowl Brood Survey	5	2.1, 2.2	Refuge	X	NA	NA
Bald Eagle Nest/Productivity Survey	4	2.1, 2.2	Refuge, State, National	X	2	3

Biological Surveys, Rice Lake NWR

Study/Survey	Priority(10 high, 1 low)	CCP Objective	Scales	FWS R3 RCP	# Runs	# Routes
Beaver Lodge/Muskrat Hut Survey	4	2.2	Refuge		1	3
Christmas Bird Count	4	2.1, 2.2	Refuge, State, National	X	1	4
North American Amphibian Monitoring Program	4	2.2	Refuge, State		3	1
Loon Productivity Monitoring (on refuge)	3	2.1, 2.2	Refuge	X	NA	NA
Wood Duck Box Program	3	2.1, 2.2	Refuge	X	1	1
Bluebird Box Program	3	2.2	Refuge		3	1
Raptor/Waterbird/Shorebird Survey (at same time as Waterfowl Surveys)	2	2.1, 2.2	Refuge	X	17	3
Fish Population Survey	2	1.8, 2.2	Refuge		1	1
Chronic Wasting Disease Monitoring	1	2.2	Refuge, State, Region		NA	NA
Statewide Loon Survey	1	2.2	State	X	1	4
Ruffed Grouse Drumming	1	2.2	Refuge		1	3
Sharptail Grouse Lek Survey (MNDNR does for us at Sandstone)	1	2.2	Refuge, State		1	1
Refuge American Woodcock Singing Ground Survey	1	2.1, 2.2	Refuge	X	1	3
Midwinter Waterfowl Survey	1	2.1, 2.2	Refuge, Region, National	X	1	1
This list was developed based on Fiscal Year 2007 funding and grant opportunities; and is expected to change before the lifetime of this plan expires due to changes in technology, future threats, funding allocation and grant opportunities.						

Appendix F: Compatibility Determinations

In accordance with the Refuge Improvement Act of 1997, no uses for which the Service has authority to regulate may be allowed on a unit of the Refuge System unless it is determined to be compatible. A compatible use is a use that, in the sound professional judgment of the refuge manager, will not materially interfere with or detract from the fulfillment of the National Wildlife Refuge System mission or the purposes of the national wildlife refuge. Managers must complete a written compatibility determination for each use, or collection of like-uses, that is signed by the manager and the Regional Chief of Refuges in the respective Service region. Draft compatibility determinations applicable to uses described in this CCP were published with the Draft CCP and EA and received 30 days of public review.

Signed compatibility determinations are on file at Rice Lake NWR for the following activities:

- Interpretation and Environmental Education
- Recreational Fishing
- Hunting
- Ceremonial use of sacred sites on Indian Point by the Mille Lacs (East Lake) Band of Ojibwe
- Archeological Investigations
- Research projects by third parties (Rice Lake NWR and Sandstone Unit)
- Research projects by third parties (Mille Lacs NWR)

- Temporary work outside existing rights-of-way
- Trapping
- Tree harvest by third parties for habitat management purposes
- Wildlife Observation and photography (including the means of access, such as automobile driving, hiking, biking, snowshoeing, cross-country skiing, canoeing, kayaking and boating and the incidental use of picnicking)

Appendix G: Compliance Requirements

Appendix G / Compliance Requirements

Rivers and Harbor Act (1899) (33 U.S.C. 403)

Section 10 of this Act requires the authorization by the U.S. Army Corps of Engineers prior to any work in, on, over, or under a navigable water of the United States.

Antiquities Act (1906)

Authorizes the scientific investigation of antiquities on Federal land and provides penalties for unauthorized removal of objects taken or collected without a permit.

Migratory Bird Treaty Act (1918)

Designates the protection of migratory birds as a Federal responsibility. This Act enables the setting of seasons, and other regulations including the closing of areas, Federal or non Federal, to the hunting of migratory birds.

Migratory Bird Conservation Act (1929)

Establishes procedures for acquisition by purchase, rental, or gift of areas approved by the Migratory Bird Conservation Commission.

Fish and Wildlife Coordination Act (1934), as amended

Requires that the Fish and Wildlife Service and State fish and wildlife agencies be consulted whenever water is to be impounded, diverted or modified under a Federal permit or license. The Service and State agency recommend measures to prevent the loss of biological resources, or to mitigate or compensate for the damage. The project proponent must take biological resource values into account and adopt justifiable protection measures to obtain maximum overall project benefits. A 1958 amendment added provisions to recognize the vital contribution of wildlife resources to the Nation and to require equal consideration and coordination of wildlife conservation with other water resources development programs. It also authorized the Secretary of Interior to provide public fishing areas and accept donations of lands and funds.

Migratory Bird Hunting and Conservation Stamp Act (1934)

Authorized the opening of part of a refuge to waterfowl hunting.

Historic Sites, Buildings and Antiquities Act (1935), as amended

Declares it a national policy to preserve historic sites and objects of national significance, including those located on refuges. Provides procedures for designation, acquisition, administration, and protection of such sites.

Refuge Revenue Sharing Act (1935), as amended

Requires revenue sharing provisions to all fee-title ownerships that are administered solely or primarily by the Secretary through the Service.

Transfer of Certain Real Property for Wildlife Conservation Purposes Act (1948)

Provides that upon a determination by the Administrator of the General Services Administration, real property no longer needed by a Federal agency can be transferred without reimbursement to the Secretary of Interior if the land has particular value for migratory birds, or to a State agency for other wildlife conservation purposes.

Federal Records Act (1950)

Directs the preservation of evidence of the government's organization, functions, policies, decisions, operations, and activities, as well as basic historical and other information.

Fish and Wildlife Act (1956)

Established a comprehensive national fish and wildlife policy and broadened the authority for acquisition and development of refuges.

Refuge Recreation Act (1962)

Allows the use of refuges for recreation when such uses are compatible with the refuge's primary purposes and when sufficient funds are available to manage the uses.

Wilderness Act (1964), as amended

Directed the Secretary of Interior, within 10 years, to review every roadless area of 5,000 or more acres and every roadless island (regardless of size) within National Wildlife Refuge and National Park Systems and to recommend to the President the suitability of each such area or island for inclusion in the National Wilderness Preservation System, with final decisions made by Congress. The Secretary of Agriculture was directed to study and recommend suitable areas in the National Forest System.

Land and Water Conservation Fund Act (1965)

Uses the receipts from the sale of surplus Federal land, outer continental shelf oil and gas sales, and other sources for land acquisition under several authorities.

National Wildlife Refuge System Administration Act (1966), as amended by the National Wildlife Refuge System Improvement Act (1997)16 U.S.C. 668dd668ee. (Refuge Administration Act)

Defines the National Wildlife Refuge System and authorizes the Secretary to permit any use of a refuge provided such use is compatible with the major purposes for which the refuge was established. The Refuge Improvement Act clearly defines a unifying mission for the Refuge System; establishes the legitimacy and appropriateness of the six priority public uses (hunting, fishing, wildlife observation and photography, or environmental education and interpretation); establishes a formal process for determining compatibility; established the responsibilities of the Secretary of Interior for managing and protecting the System; and requires a Comprehensive Conservation Plan for each refuge by the year 2012. This Act amended portions of the Refuge Recreation Act and National Wildlife Refuge System Administration Act of 1966.

National Historic Preservation Act (1966), as amended

Establishes as policy that the Federal Government is to provide leadership in the preservation of the nation's prehistoric and historic resources. Section 106 requires Federal agencies to consider impacts their undertakings could have on historic properties; Section 110 requires Federal agencies to manage historic properties, e.g., to document historic properties prior to destruction or damage; Section 101 requires Federal agencies to consider Indian tribal values in historic preservation programs, and requires each Federal agency to establish a program leading to inventory of all historic properties on its land.

Architectural Barriers Act (1968)

Requires federally owned, leased, or funded buildings and facilities to be accessible to persons with disabilities.

National Environmental Policy Act (1969)

Requires the disclosure of the environmental impacts of any major Federal action significantly affecting the quality of the human environment.

Uniform Relocation and Assistance and Real Property Acquisition Policies Act (1970), as amended

Provides for uniform and equitable treatment of persons who sell their homes, businesses, or farms to the Service. The Act requires that any purchase offer be no less than the fair market value of the property.

Endangered Species Act (1973)

Requires all Federal agencies to carry out programs for the conservation of endangered and threatened species.

Rehabilitation Act (1973)

Requires programmatic accessibility in addition to physical accessibility for all facilities and programs funded by the Federal government to ensure that anybody can participate in any program.

Archaeological and Historic Preservation Act (1974)

Directs the preservation of historic and archaeological data in Federal construction projects.

Clean Water Act (1977)

Requires consultation with the Corps of Engineers (404 permits) for major wetland modifications.

Surface Mining Control and Reclamation Act (1977) as amended (Public Law 95-87) (SMCRA)

Regulates surface mining activities and reclamation of coal-mined lands. Further regulates the coal industry by designating certain areas as unsuitable for coal mining operations.

Executive Order 11988 (1977)

Each Federal agency shall provide leadership and take action to reduce the risk of flood loss and minimize the impact of floods on human safety, and preserve the natural and beneficial values served by the floodplains.

Executive Order 11990

Executive Order 11990 directs Federal agencies to (1) minimize destruction, loss, or degradation of wetlands and (2) preserve and enhance the natural and beneficial values of wetlands when a practical alternative exists.

Executive Order 12372 (Intergovernmental Review of Federal Programs)

Directs the Service to send copies of the Environmental Assessment to State Planning Agencies for review.

American Indian Religious Freedom Act (1978)

Directs agencies to consult with native traditional religious leaders to determine appropriate policy changes necessary to protect and preserve American Indian religious cultural rights and practices.

Fish and Wildlife Improvement Act (1978)

Improves the administration of fish and wildlife programs and amends several earlier laws including the Refuge Recreation Act, the National Wildlife Refuge System Administration Act, and the Fish and Wildlife Act of 1956. It authorizes the Secretary to accept gifts and bequests of real and personal property on behalf of the United States. It also authorizes the use of volunteers on Service projects and appropriations to carry out a volunteer program.

Archaeological Resources Protection Act (1979), as amended

Protects materials of archaeological interest from unauthorized removal or destruction and requires Federal managers to develop plans and schedules to locate archaeological resources.

Federal Farmland Protection Policy Act (1981), as amended

Minimizes the extent to which Federal programs contribute to the unnecessary and irreversible conversion of farmland to nonagricultural uses.

Emergency Wetlands Resources Act (1986)

Promotes the conservation of migratory waterfowl and offsets or prevents the serious loss of wetlands by the acquisition of wetlands and other essential habitats.

Federal Noxious Weed Act (1990)

Requires the use of integrated management systems to control or contain undesirable plant species, and an interdisciplinary approach with the cooperation of other Federal and State agencies.

Native American Graves Protection and Repatriation Act (1990)

Requires Federal agencies and museums to inventory, determine ownership of, and repatriate cultural items under their control or possession.

Americans With Disabilities Act (1992)

Prohibits discrimination in public accommodations and services.

Executive Order 12898 (1994)

Establishes environmental justice as a Federal government priority and directs all Federal agencies to make environmental justice part of their mission. Environmental justice calls for fair distribution of environmental hazards.

Executive Order 12996 Management and General Public Use of the National Wildlife Refuge System (1996)

Defines the mission, purpose, and priority public uses of the National Wildlife Refuge System. It also presents four principles to guide management of the System.

Executive Order 13007 Indian Sacred Sites (1996)

Directs Federal land management agencies to accommodate access to and ceremonial use of Indian sacred sites by Indian religious practitioners, avoid adversely affecting the physical integrity of such sacred sites, and where appropriate, maintain the confidentiality of sacred sites.

National Wildlife Refuge System Improvement Act (1997)

Considered the "Organic Act of the National Wildlife Refuge System. Defines the mission of the System, designates priority wildlife-dependent public uses, and calls for comprehensive refuge planning. Section 6 requires the Service to make a determination of compatibility of existing, new and changing uses of Refuge land; and Section 7 requires the Service to identify and describe the archaeological and cultural values of the refuge.

National Wildlife Refuge System Volunteer and Community Partnership Enhancement Act (1998)

Amends the Fish and Wildlife Act of 1956 to promote volunteer programs and community partnerships for the benefit of national wildlife refuges, and for other purposes.

National Trails System Act

Assigns responsibility to the Secretary of Interior and thus the Service to protect the historic and recreational values of congressionally designated National Historic Trail sites.

Treasury and General Government Appropriations Act of 2001 (Public Law 106-554)

In December 2002, Congress required federal agencies to publish their own guidelines for ensuring and maximizing the quality, objectivity, utility, and integrity of information that they disseminate to the public (44 U.S.C. 3502). The amended language is included in Section 515(a). The Office of Budget and Management (OMB) directed agencies to develop their own guidelines to address the requirements of the law. The Department of the Interior instructed bureaus to prepare separate guidelines on how they would apply the Act. The U.S. Fish and Wildlife Service has developed "Information Quality Guidelines" to address the law.

Cultural Resources and Historic Preservation

The National Wildlife Refuge System Improvement Act of 1997, Section 6, requires the Service to make a determination of compatibility of existing, new and changing uses of Refuge land; and Section 7 requires the Service to identify and describe the archaeological and cultural values of the refuge.

The National Historic Preservation Act (NHPA), Section 106, requires Federal agencies to consider impacts their undertakings could have on historic properties; Section 110 requires Federal agencies to manage historic properties, e.g., to document historic properties prior to destruction or damage; Section 101 requires Federal agencies consider Indian tribal values in historic preservation programs, and requires each Federal agency to establish a program leading to inventory of all historic properties on its land.

The Archaeological Resources Protection Act of 1979 (ARPA) prohibits unauthorized disturbance of archeological resources on Federal and Indian land; and other matters. Section 10 requires establishing "a program to increase public awareness" of archeological resources. Section 14 requires plans to survey lands and a schedule for surveying lands with "the most scientifically valuable archaeological resources." This Act requires protection of all archeological sites more than 100 years old (not just sites meeting the criteria for the National Register) on Federal land, and requires archeological investigations on Federal land be performed in the public interest by qualified persons.

The Native American Graves Protection and Repatriation Act of 1990 (NAGPRA) imposes serious delays on a project when human remains or other cultural items are encountered in the absence of a plan.

The American Indian Religious Freedom Act (AIRFA) iterates the right of Native Americans to free exercise of traditional religions and use of sacred places.

EO 13007, Indian Sacred Sites (1996), directs Federal agencies to accommodate access to and ceremonial use, to avoid adverse effects and avoid blocking access, and to enter into early consultation.

Collier Agreement

Copy

Collier Agreement

See pg. 3

June 4, 1935

Mr. John Collier, Commissioner,
    Bureau of Indian Affairs,
        Department of the Interior,
            Washington, D. C.

            Attention: Mr. Ward Shepard.

Dear Sir:

    Subject: Cooperative solution of the conflict between
the interests of the Indian Service and the Bureau of Biological
Survey in the Egg Lake region of Becker County, Minnesota, with
reference to their respective projects.

    As agreed at the informal conference in Mr. Shepard's of-
fice between Mr. Shepard and Mr. Burns of the Indian Service and
Mr. Salyer and Mr. Dieffenbach of the Biological Survey, I am
presenting herewith the basis for a cooperative agreement to the
interests of both parties in the development of their respective
projects which overlap in one instance.

    There is attached an outline map of Becker County upon
which has been indicated in red the boundaries of the White
Earth Indian Reservation. In green are shown the maximum boundaries of the area in which the Biological Survey is interested
in developing as a migratory waterfowl sanctuary; the lands col-
ored yellow are the lands in which the State Conservation Department of Minnesota is interested in maintaining as a State forest
and which they prescribed to the Indian Service but relinquish to
the Biological Survey inasmuch as the Survey has agreed to permit
them to extend their reforestation operations onto these lands
when they are acquired by the Biological Survey.

    On this same map, the lands of J. E. Hamilton, which form
the nucleus of our proposed project in the north, are outlined
in blue. Mr. Hamilton has indicated that he will relinquish these
lands to the survey only, because the Survey will continue the
area as a wildlife refuge, which constitutes Mr. Hamilton's original interest in the property.

    The area shaded pink on the same map shows the extent of
the area already optioned by the Indian Service and on which the

Collier Agreement (continued)

CO;Y

-2-

Biological Survey wishes to secure a release from the Indian Service in order to develop the project to its greatest scientific capacity for migratory waterfowl which development, incidentally, will also be of the greatest benefit to the resident Indians of the vicinity.

From the standpoint of the Biological Survey, the proposed project forms a very definite link in the series of migratory waterfowl refuges being established by the Biological Survey throughout the great flight lane known as the Mississippi Flyway. Tracts suitable for such refuges are not readily found because of the need for adequate food and dependable water supply. No one, we believe, will question the outstanding value of the Egg Lake region from that standpoint.

In order to properly develop the lakes and establish ideal conditions suitable for migratory birds, it is necessary that the Biological Survey control the Egg Lake River Valley. It is planned to construct some small dams stabilizing the water in the many lakes of the area and thus insure better growing conditions, especially for the wild rice. The Indian Service is mainly interested in this same area in view of the excellent rice bed found on Little Rice Lake.

In the aforementioned conference, it was the thought of Mr. Shepard and Mr. Burns that the Indian Service could well afford to release their options in this area to the Biological Survey, in return for the specific privileges to be granted to the Indians of this agency by the Biological Survey and herewith enumerated:

1. That the Indians be given priority in ricing privileges not only in the area where the interests of the two agencies overlap, but also on the much greater area which the Biological Survey is taking over in this region; namely, Flat Lake, Tamarac Lake, Pine Lake, Big Rice Lake, Height of Land Lake, Black Bird Lake, and smaller lakes too numerous to mention.

2. The Biological Survey further agrees to give the resident Indians of the agency priority in the matter of trapping rights in its entire project. The Biological Survey reserves the right at all times to preserve a minimum breeding stock of fur-bearing animals on the area. It is suggested that the Biological Survey set up a number of trapping units over these prolific fur-producing waters, and that the Indian Service assign certain Indian families or groups the right to trap specific units.

3. The Biological Survey further agrees to train in rotation a series of young Indian men of high character along the most

Collier Agreement (continued)

<u>COPY</u>

-3-

modern lines of game management. The Indian Service agrees to pay their salaries, and the Biological Survey will, through its resident biologists on the tract, give them specific practical training along modern game management lines. The philosophy is that these men will be transferred to other Indian projects as soon as they become proficient, and others will take their place.

4. The Biological Survey further agrees to use Indian CCC labor in the development of the project.

5. The Biological Survey further agrees to protect and guarantee to the Indian Service the <u>ricing privileges</u> on the Biological Survey's purchase unit <u>in Aitkin County known as the Rice Lake Migratory Waterfowl Refuge unit</u>. This <u>lake</u> produces annually from 90 to 100 tons of wild rice, and the granting of priority to the Indians for harvesting this will be decidedly to the advantage of this people. At this time, the Biological Survey is engaged in constructing two small dams to stabilize the water levels in this lake, with a view of perpetuating this great rice bed. It is feared that if another year goes by, with the attendant lowering of water levels before the rice matures, this great bed may be permanently and seriously injured.

At present, there exists an arbitrary agreement between the Indian Service and the Minnesota State Conservation Department adopting a boundary line between the two projects separating the eastern halves of the two townships, T142N, Range 39W, and T141N, Range 39W, from the original established civic township governments. The Sugar Bush Township is all but annihilated by the present Indian boundaries. The entrance of the Biological Survey into the picture would permit this area to be closed out entirely. This is most important in view of the fact that the County Boards of both Becker and Mahnoman Counties have made their delinquent tax abatement resolutions dependent upon the Government's buying all of Townships 141N and 142N.

Considered from all angles and the mutual interests of both parties to this agreement, it seems certain that the entrance of the Biological Survey into the picture and the consummation of the Survey migratory waterfowl project here will serve to round out the unfulfilled situations in the whole set-up, and that is is to the mutual advantage of both parties to enter into this agreement.

It is a recognized fact that the harvesting of wild rice by the Indian method does not destroy the annual yield of this plant; and the annual yield of this harvest to the Indians of the Egg Lake region will be greatly enhanced not only because all of the water area of the entire refuge unit will become available to

Collier Agreement (continued)

<u>COPY</u>

—¼—

the Indians for ricing purposes after it has been acquired by the
Biological Survey, but also because the engineering development
by the Survey will establish permanent water levels which are most
beneficial to the natural production of wild rice. Properly-
designed dams will also bring into rice production the present
rather dry savanna type of meadow valley of the Egg and Ottor Tail
Rivers.

In the development of the area to its best condition, there
will be a continuous demand for Indian labor, and the area will
at the same time serve as a training school for Indian game managers. As stated before, the rich fur harvest of this region will
be made available to the Indians.

Enclosure.

      (Signed)   W. C. Henderson
                       Acting Chief,
                       Bureau of Biological Survey.

      (Signed)   John Collier
                       John Collier, Commissioner,
                       Bureau of Indian Affairs.

Appendix H: Literature Cited

Literature Cited

Crozier, G.E., and G.J. Niemi. 2003. Using patch and landscape variables to model bird abundance in a naturally heterogeneous landscape. Canadian Journal of Zoology 81:441-452.

Dai, X., Boutton, T.W., Hailemichael, M., Ansley, R.J., Jessup, K.E. 2006. Soil Carbon and Nitrogen Storage in Response to Fire in a Temperate Mixed-Grass Savanna. J. Environ Qual. 35:1620-1628.

Degraaf. R., Yamasaki, M., 2003. Options for managing early-successional forest and shrubland bird habitats in northeastern United States. Forest Ecology and Management 185, 179-191.

Green. J., 1995. Birds and Forest, a Management and Conservation Guide. State of Minnesota, Department of Natural Resources. 182 pages.

Herkert, James R., Robert E Szafoni, Vernon M. Kleen, and John E. Schwegman. 1993. Habitat establishment, enhancement and management for forest and grassland birds in Illinois. Division of Natural Heritage, Illinois

Holling, C.S. and G.K. Meffe. 1996. Command and control and the pathology of natural resource management. Conservation Biology 10:328-337.

Department of Conservation, Natural Heritage Technical Publication #1, Springfield, Illinois. Northern Prairie Wildlife Research Center Online. http://www.npwrc.usgs.gov/resource/birds/manbook/manbook.htm (Version 16JUL97).

Jarvenpa, R., 1971a, Political Entrenchment in an Ojibwa Wild Rice Economy. Journal of the Minnesota Academy of Science (37(2-3):66-71.

Jarvenpa, R., 1971b, the Wild Rice Gatherers of Rice Lake, Minnesota: A Brief Note on Cultural Historical Indicators. Minnesota Archaeologist 31(3):71-105.

Johnson, C., 1945, "Early History of Rice Lake National Wildlife Refuge." On file at Rice Lake NWR. Minnesota.

Johnson, C.M., 1992a, A Phase I Cultural Resource Survey of a Proposed Headquarters Building Site, Aitkin County, Minnesota. Institute for Minnesota Archaeology Reports of Investigations No. 225 prepared for U.S. Fish & Wildlife Service.

Johnson, C.M., 1992b, Phase I and II Archaeological Investigations of Sixteen Project Areas in Minnesota. Institute for Minnesota Archaeology Reports of Investigations No. 177 prepared for U.S. Fish & Wildlife Service.

Johnson, E., 1989, Cultural Resources Investigation: Rice Lake National Wildlife Refuge. Institute for Minnesota Archaeology Reports of Investigations No. 35 prepared for U.S. Fish & Wildlife Service.

Johnson, E., 1990, Cultural Resources Investigation II: Rice Lake National Wildlife Refuge. Institute for Minnesota Archaeology Reports of Investigations No. 72 prepared for U.S. Fish & Wildlife Service.

King, Thomas F. Cultural Resource Laws & Practice. 1998: AltaMira Press, Walnut Creek.

Lambeck, R.J. 1997. Focal species: a multi-species umbrella for nature conservation. Conservation Biology 11:849-856.

Lapp, Christopher. 1995. Rice Lake National Wildlife Refuge holds record concentration of waterfowl. The Loon. Vol 67. Pages 38-40.

Minnesota Department of Natural Resources, 2006. Tomorrow's Habitat for the Wild and Rare: An Action Plan for Minnesota Wildlife, Comprehensive Wildlife Conservation Strategy. Division of Ecological Services, Minnesota Department of Natural Resources.

Minnesota Forest Resources Council. 2001. Minnesota's White Pine in the Future. Landscape Technical Document (LT-0301a). 44 pages. On the Internet at http://www.iic.state.mn.us/finfo/luse/harvest.htm.

Minnesota Pollution Control Agency. 2005. Sources of mercury pollution and methylmercury contamination of fish in Minnesota. Pollution prevention & sustainability fact sheet #4-06. 3 pp. On the Internet at http://www.pca.state.mn.us/publications/p-p2s4-06.pdf

National Assessment Synthesis Team, *Climate Change Impacts on the United States: The Potential Consequences of Climate Variability and Change,* US Global Change Research Program, Washington DC, 2000

Norrgard, Ray. 2005. Wetland complexity, how to recover ducks: key action for improving habitat. Minnesota Conservation Volunteer. September-October. Page 22.

Ollendorf, A.L., 2000b, Emergency Water Well and Pipeline Replacement, Rice Lake National Wildlife Refuge near McGregor, Aitkin County, Minnesota. Phase 1 Site Identification and Construction Monitoring. HDR Engineering, Inc. report prepared for U.S. Fish & Wildlife Service.

Schroeder, Richard L., Wayne J. King, and John E. Cornely. 1998. Selecting habitat management strategies on refuges. Information and Technology Report, USGS/BRD/ITR – 1998-003. U.S. Geological Survey.

Appendix I: Distribution List

Distribution List

The following is a list of government officials and offices and private organizations that received the CCP. Individuals who requested a copy of the Draft also received the document. Others on the Refuge's planning mailing list and those listed in Chapter 6 of the Environmental Assessment received a summary of the CCP and a notice of where a full copy could be obtained. The availability of the CCP was announced in the Federal Register and a press release was sent to local newspapers.

Elected Officials

- Senator Norm Coleman
- Senator Amy Klobuchar
- Representative James Oberstar

American Indian Tribes

- Mille Lacs Band of Ojibwe

Federal Agencies

- U.S. Army Corps of Engineers, Sandy Lake Recreation Area
- U.S. Department of Justice, Federal Bureau of Prisons

State Agencies

- Minnesota Department of Natural Resources
- Minnesota Department of Natural Resources, Division of Forestry
- Minnesota Department of Transportation, MN DOT Truck Station

Local Government and Public Services

- Aitkin County Commissioner-3rd District
- Aitkin County Land Department
- Aitkin County Soil and Water Conservation District
- McGregor Public Library
- Relief Association, McGregor Volunteer Fire Department

Non-government Organizations

- Audubon Center of the North Woods
- Audubon Society of the District of Columbia
- Big Sandy Area Lakes Watershed Management Project
- Bluewater Network
- CCC Alumni Chapter 119
- Defenders of Wildlife
- Institute for Policy Research, Northwestern University
- National Fish and Wildlife Foundation
- National Trappers Association, Inc.
- National Wildlife Federation
- National Wildlife Refuge Association
- PEER Refuge Keeper
- Sierra Club - Midwest Office
- The Conservation Fund, Arlington, Virginia
- The Wilderness Society
- Wilderness Watch

Appendix J: List of Preparers

List of Preparers

Walt Ford, Refuge Manager, Rice Lake National Wildlife Refuge

Mary Stefanski, Former Refuge Manager, Rice Lake National Wildlife Refuge

Michelle McDowell, Biologist, Rice Lake National Wildlife Refuge

John Schomaker, Refuge Planner, Region 3, USFWS

H. John Dobrovolny, Regional Historic Preservation Officer, Region 3, USFWS

Gabriel DeAlessio, Biologist/GIS, Region 3, USFWS

Jane Hodgins, Technical Writer/Editor, Region 3

Appendix K: Response to Comments Received on the Draft Comprehensive Conservation Plan and Environmental Assessment

Habitat Management Topics

1. *The Minnesota Department of Natural Resources concurs with the plan. The plan would be enhanced by a fuller discussion of planned partnerships in the managing of open land adjacent to the Kimberly Marsh Wildlife Management Area.*

   Response: The Refuge continues to appreciate the cooperation and partnership it experiences with the Minnesota DNR. Additions have been incorporated into the Final CCP to reflect the ongoing partnership and our joint activities.

2. *The Refuge should harvest hay from old crop fields to enhance wildlife viewing opportunities. The revenue from haying would benefit the Refuge. The reasoning behind conversion of the old fields to forest is not clear.*

   Response: The Refuge would hay to enhance, support, and contribute to established wildlife management objectives. Haying does not support the purpose of the Refuge for providing for migrating birds. The fields converted to forest will benefit forest-interior birds by increasing the block size of the Refuge forest as described in Objective 1.1. Revenue from haying would not be retained by the Refuge and would not, therefore, directly benefit the Refuge.

3. *The Refuge should have initiated discussion with other organizations, i.e.: Ducks Unlimited, Minnesota Deer Hunters Association, Grouse Society, Turkey Federation, and Minnesota Waterfowl Association, to achieve more balanced management objectives that aren't slanted towards songbirds.*

   Response: The Refuge mission as defined by the Mission of the National Wildlife Refuge System is to "...conserve a diversity of fish, wildlife, and plants..." as well as "Develop and maintain a network of habitats for migratory birds . . . to meet important life history needs of these species across their ranges." As such, the Refuge is managing for a wide assortment of migratory birds within their native range. Refuge management objectives will benefit waterfowl as well as songbirds. Forest restoration will also provide long-term benefits to ruffed grouse, whitetail deer, and wild turkey (if/when they become resident wildlife).

4. *The water level in Rice Lake should be maintained at the highest level possible in the fall to retain waterfowl, which would benefit hunting and the local economy. Water levels should not be manipulated to benefit only ricing. The Refuge should consult with Ducks Unlimited for assistance with lake management.*

   Response: The intent of water level variation as described in the plan is to ensure the long-term viability of a healthy rice crop, which will benefit both migrating fall waterfowl and ricing. The Refuge consulted with Ducks Unlimited and other experts in the past. As the Refuge implements and evaluates the results of the direction specified in the CCP, the consultations will continue.

5. *After a prescribed fire exotic invasives move in and native plants are lost forever.*

   Response: Prescribed fire benefits native plants, which have evolved with fire. The Refuge's prescribed fire operations are conducted in a way that minimizes the introduction of exotics. Fuel and soil moisture are considered before initiating a burn.

6. *The Refuge should burn the islands within the bog, which will improve sharptail grouse habitat.*

   Response: Periodic burning of the islands is expected. Although no extraordinary efforts will be used to prevent burning of islands, care will be taken to not burn the islands as frequently as the open bog. Frequent burns will be necessary to control brush in the open bog which will be beneficial for sharptail grouse.

7. *The Refuge should consider abandoning or removing existing ditches and water control structures altogether. The rhythm of the year's variation has served us well in other rice beds.*

   Response: The Refuge did consider removing the water control structure, but chose to enter a test phase of allowing natural variation of water levels with the structure open, but in place. The Refuge is reluctant to remove the structure, an expensive operation, without knowing the result of natural variation.

Wildlife-Dependent Recreation Topics

8. *Hunting and trapping should not be allowed on the Refuge because it kills, harms, and disturbs wildlife.*

   Response: We understand some citizens' concern with hunting and trapping on national wildlife refuges. Rice Lake NWR, as well as the entire National Wildlife Refuge System, is guided by laws enacted by Congress and the President as well as policy derived from those laws. The 1997 National Wildlife Refuge System Improvement Act identifies hunting as one of six priority public uses to be facilitated when compatible with the purposes of a refuge and the mission of the Refuge System. Hunting is consistent with the purposes of the Refuge. While National Wildlife Refuges are managed first and foremost for wildlife, the focus is on perpetuating populations, not individuals. Hunting and trapping does adversely affect individual animals, but is allowed when it will not threaten the perpetuation of the population.

9. *The Draft CCP does not meet the requirements of the National Wildlife Refuge System Improvement Act of 1997 because insufficient investigation of biological integrity, diversity and environmental health were undertaken prior to plan preparation. Rigorous biological analyses, with conclusions published in a NEPA document subject to public review, need to be conducted of wildlife populations to ensure that there is a surplus, before making any compatibility determinations about the killing of wildlife.*

   Response: The Draft CCP listed a number of wildlife surveys and censuses that are conducted at Rice Lake that in sum provide an adequate basis for making informed decisions on the compatibility of hunting and trapping. In addition, the year-to-year trapping records themselves, and long-term trends in these numbers, furnish valuable information that can be used in opening or closing seasons. Recognizing that it does not have limitless budgetary and personnel resources to conduct ideal surveys that would yield perfect information on wildlife population sizes, the Refuge and Service use adaptive resource management, several features of which are monitoring, feedback, flexibility, and making adjustments in midcourse whenever the data point in that direction.

10. *The Service cannot continue to endorse hunting on any National Wildlife Refuge without analyzing its impact as required by the NWR-SIA of 1997 and NEPA through an Environmental Impact Statement.*

    Response: The comment references a legal complaint filed in Federal court, The Fund et al. v. Williams et al., Civ. No. 03-677. The complaint has been responded to by the Service and is under evaluation by the court as of this writing. The complaint does not specifically discuss the hunting program on Rice Lake NWR. See the previous response, and Chapter 3 of the CCP, for the Service's current approach toward hunting on Rice Lake NWR.

11. *There are environmental education opportunities with the East Lake and McGregor schools.*

    Response: The Refuge will pursue these and other environmental education opportunities as the plan is implemented.

Native American Topics

12. *There is a desire for federal recognition of the Rice Lake Band of Ojibwe.*

    Response: Federal recognition of a tribe is outside the Service's authority.

13. *The Rice Lake Band of Ojibwe desires a more active role in management of the Refuge.*

    Response: The Refuge welcomes the input of the Rice Lake Band among the many factors that it must consider in making management decisions. Any formal agreement with the Rice Lake Band would require federal tribal recognition.

Other Topics

14. *Removing the buildings from Indian Point at an estimated cost of $3.9 million at a time of low funding does not seem like a wise use of funds, and $3.9 million seems like a very high estimate.*

Response: Moving the buildings will only be done when funding is available. The estimate for the project was provided by the Service's Engineering Division. Their estimate was based on their experience with similar projects and considers inflation.

15. *The Refuge should consider Native American concerns, habitat for threatened birds, and water quality as it implements the plan. Access should be limited to protect the land and animals.*

   Response: The CCP and its implementation will consider all the values noted. Access is only permitted when compatible with the purpose of the Refuge and the mission of the System.

16. *Prescribed fire results in an unacceptable change in air quality.*

   Response: Section 4.1.6 of the Environmental Assessment describes the actions the Refuge will take to mitigate the impacts on air quality in its prescribed fire operation.

17. *All federal agencies have an on-going obligation to ensure that Endangered Species Act listed species are not jeopardized by their actions.*

   Response: An Intra-Service Section 7 Biological Evaluation has been completed and is part of the formal record of the planning process.

18. *The Service should trade the Sandstone Unit for the Kimberly Marsh Wildlife Management Area.*

   Response: The concept of trading Refuge tracts with the Minnesota DNR lands was developed with the objective of simplifying management where Service and the DNR have small parcels intermixed. The Service and the DNR will consider exchanges anywhere in the State. An exchange of lands requires approval by both the Service and the DNR.

19. *The Refuge should not withdraw the Wilderness recommendation as proposed in the preferred alternative.*

   Response: The recommendation to consider a portion of the Refuge as Wilderness occurred in 1973. The recommendation has not been acted upon during the interceding 34 years. Refuge staff have concluded that the recommendation is no longer appropriate because the area fails to meet numerous criteria that were established to determine Wilderness suitability: it is less than 5,000 acres in size; human alterations to the habitat are readily apparent on portions of the area; it offers little opportunity for primitive recreational activities other than hunting; and it does not contain significant ecological, geological, scientific, educational, scenic, or historical features. Removing the Wilderness recommendation will allow for a complete range of management options to restore altered and/or degraded wildlife habitat.

20. *The CCP is good and the efforts of the Refuge staff are appreciated.*

   Response: The Service and Refuge appreciate the endorsement of the plan and their efforts.

www.ingramcontent.com/pod-product-compliance
Lightning Source LLC
Chambersburg PA
CBHW081212280526
45787CB00006B/2392